FOR INFORMATION:

If you need help to understand the guidance in this booklet contact your local environmental health department.

"এই পুস্তিকার নির্দেশাবলী বুঝতে যদি আপনার সাহায্যের দরকার হয়, তাহলে আপনার স্থানীয় পরিবেশ স্বাস্থ্য বিভাগ (Environmental Health Department)-এর সঙ্গে যোগাযোগ করুন।"

(Bengali)

આ નાની પુસ્તિકામાં આપેલ માર્ગદર્શન સમજવામાં તમને જો મદદની જરૂર હોય તો મહેરબાની કરીને તમારા સ્થાનિક એનવાઈરનમન્ટલ હેલ્થ ડિપાર્ટમન્ટને (પર્યાવરણજન્ય આરોગ્ય ખાતાનો) સંપર્ક સાધશો।

(Gujarati)

"ਜੇ ਤੁਹਾਨੂੰ ਇਸ ਕਿਤਾਬਚੇ ਦੀ ਰਹਿਨੁਮਾਈ ਸਮਝਣ ਵਿਚ ਮੱਦਦ ਚਾਹੀਦੀ ਹੈ ਤਾਂ ਆਪਣੇ ਸਥਾਨਕ ਐਨਵਾਇਰਨਮੈਂਟਲ ਹੈਲਥ ਡਿਪਾਰਟਮੈਂਟ (Environmental Health Department) ਨਾਲ ਸੰਪਰਕ ਕਰੋ।"

(Punjabi)

"اگر آپ کو اِس کتابچہ میں دی گئی رہنمائی کو سمجھنے میں مدد کی ضرورت ہے تو اپنے مقامی انوائرمینٹل ہیلتھ ڈپارٹمنٹ سے رابطہ قائم کیجے"۔

(Urdu)

如果您想瞭解關於本手冊的詳細指引，請向您當地的環保處洽詢。

(Chinese)

«Αν χρειαστείτε βοήθεια στην κατανόηση των οδηγιών που περιέχονται σε αυτό το βιβλιαράκι, επικοινωνήστε με τη Διεύθυνση Περιβαλλοντικής Υγιεινής της περιοχής σας».

(Greek)

Eğer bu elkitabındaki açıklamaları anlayabilmek için yardıma ihtiyaç duyuyorsanız, yerel Çevre Sağlığı Dairenize başvurunuz.

(Turkish)

Industry Guide to Good Hygiene Practice:

Markets and Fairs Guide

Regulations 1995

Chadwick House
Group Ltd.

ISBN 1 902423 00 3

PUBLISHED BY CHADWICK HOUSE GROUP LTD.

Chadwick Court
15 Hatfields
London SE1 8DJ

Tel: 0171 827 5882 Main switchboard: 0171 928 6006 Fax: 0171 827 9930

Chadwick House Group Ltd is the trading subsidiary of the Chartered Institute of Environmental Health (CIEH), the professional and educational body for those who work in environmental health in England, Wales and Northern Ireland. Founded in 1883, the Chartered Institute has charitable status and its primary function is the promotion of knowledge and understanding of environmental health issues. A Royal Charter was granted in 1984. The majority of CIEH members work as Environmental Health Officers in local authorities; some work in central government, academia, as independent consultants and in positions overseas.

Chadwick House Group Ltd manages the development and promotion of these qualifications. The company is a major publisher of environmental health publications, including the weekly Environmental Health News, the monthly journal, Environmental Health and the food safety quarterly bulletin, Food Forum. The company also publishes a variety of books, videos and reports on food safety, health & safety, housing and environmental protection.

More information about the CIEH can be accessed through the CIEH Website at www.cieh.org.uk/

Preface

This Industry Guide to Good Hygiene Practice gives advice to food businesses operating within markets and fairs on how to comply with the Food Safety (General Food Hygiene) Regulations 1995 and the Food Safety (Temperature Control) Regulations 1995. This is an official guide to the Regulations which has been developed in accordance with article 5 of the EC Directive on the hygiene of foodstuffs (93/43/EEC).

Whilst this Guide is not legally binding, officers from food authorities must give it due consideration when they enforce the Regulations. It is hoped that the information which this Guide contains will help you to both meet your legal obligations and to ensure food safety.

Acknowledgements

The National Association of British Market Authorities wishes to thank the following organisations, and their representatives, who formed the working group which was responsible for the development of this Guide.

The Association of Private Market Operators (APMO)
Representative: Michael Felton & Wendy Hobday

The Institute of Market Officers (IMO)
Representative: Ian Hill

The Mobile and Outside Caterers Association
Representative: Bob Fox

The National Market Traders' Federation (NMTF)
Representative: John Burton*

The Showmen's Guild of Great Britain
Representative: Ernest Johnson

The development of the Guide was co-ordinated by Krys Zasada (National Association of British Market Authorities) whilst the drafting of the document was facilitated by Bernadette Kitching, Janet Gingell, Dorothy Laycock and Julia Strachan (Environmental Health Officers, Sheffield City Council).

In addition, thanks are extended to John Barnes, Alistair Edwards and Peter Martin (Department of Health) and Clare Cunningham and David Lock (Local Authorities Co-ordinating Body on Food and Trading Standards) for their advice and support. The working group also appreciate the valuable responses received during the public consultation exercise.

Finally, thanks to all those who used their keyboard and software skills to produce the Guide, particularly Kath Goodwin, Andrew Chappell, Debbie Askham and Tracey Bamford.

*This Guide was completed after John's untimely death on August 17th 1997. His contribution to its development is greatly valued.

Contents

Part 1　　　　　　Introduction

The purpose of this Guide is to provide food businesses operating within markets and fairs, with information and practical advice on how to comply with the Food Safety (General Food Hygiene) Regulations 1995 (hereinafter referred to as the Regulations), the Food Safety (Temperature Control) Regulations 1995 (hereinafter referred to as the Temperature Regulations), and the equivalent for Northern Ireland.

The National Association of British Market Authorities initiated the establishment of a working group of various organisations, representing markets and fairs operators and traders, which prepared the Guide. The organisations involved, and their representatives, are listed within the Acknowledgements.

Whilst this Guide provides a recommended means of complying with the law it is not a legal requirement to follow its advice. However, enforcement officers must give due consideration to the 'Guide to Compliance' sections of the Guide when assessing compliance with the Regulations and Temperature Regulations. It may, of course, be possible for a business to demonstrate to enforcers that it has achieved the objectives of these Regulations in other ways.

It must also be stressed that whilst the standards within this document are based on practical knowledge of the food industry and conditions necessary to ensure hygiene in the production of food, it is ultimately for the courts to interpret the legislation.

Food Businesses Covered by this Guide
This Guide is intended to cover food businesses operating **within markets and fairs only, mobile vehicles and street traders.** These will include:

Wholesale Markets	*Retail Markets*	*Catering at Markets and Fairs*
● Fruit & vegetable merchants	● Bakers/Confectioners	● Restaurants
● "Cash & Carry" food outlets	● Butchers	● Cafes
● Bakers/confectioners	● Poulterers	● Hot Food Take Aways
● Wholesalers not covered by 'product specific' legislation	● Fishmongers	● Sandwiches
	● Delicatessens	● Candy Floss
	● Grocers	● Doughnuts
	● Health Foods	● Hot Potatoes/Chestnuts
	● Sweets	● Ice-Cream
	● Frozen Foods	

Within the markets and fairs sector the above businesses could be operated from permanent or temporary stalls, mobile vehicles, or handcarts.

Note 1　　There are areas of overlap with other industry guides (e.g. tents and marquees used for catering purposes at large outdoor events - Catering Guide; and baking operations - Bakers Guide). Where possible, sufficient detail has been included in this Guide to cover all food businesses operating from markets and fairs. Other guides, which will have consistent requirements, may be used as an alternative source of information. This Guide does not cover commercial catering activities from domestic premises or information on vending machines. Consult the Catering Guide and Vending Guide respectively for information on these operations.

Note 2　　Some food businesses may already be covered by product specific "vertical" food hygiene legislation (e.g. wholesale fishery products, red meat and poultry meat). The specific requirements of these wholesale businesses are **not** included in this Guide although some general requirements such as training for food handlers will apply to them.

Note 3　　Other non-food related legislation (e.g. Health and Safety, Consumer Protection, Environmental Protection) with which food businesses must comply is also excluded from the Guide. However, consideration will need to be given to such other legislation for premises, practices and personnel. For example, The Workplace (Health, Safety and Welfare) Regulations 1992 give details on the provision of sanitary conveniences and washing facilities.

Note 4 Although **Market and Fair Operators** are not food businesses for the purposes of the legislation, any communal facilities they provide for food businesses under the terms of their lease or agreement should comply with the Regulations and Temperature Regulations. A separate section is included in this Guide giving advice on the standard of services that are provided to food traders.

The Department of Health, The Welsh Office and the Scottish Office have all produced leaflets which explain the role of Environmental Health and Trading Standards Services in enforcing food law and in helping you to produce safe food.

These leaflets describe:

- What to expect when your business is inspected; and

- What to do if you think the outcome of an inspection is wrong or not fair.

They are available free of charge from your local Environmental Health and Trading Standards Services.

How to use this Guide

Simply work through the numbered headings below and see which apply to your business. The relevant page/section number is given for each area.

Turn to the relevant page/section for details of what the law requires, how to comply with the law, and additional information on "good practice".

The traders' checklists and appendices may be freely photocopied for use by businesses but the remainder of the Guide is subject to copyright.

N.B. It is NOT a legal requirement to follow advice on "good practice".

1. **Food Safety - Controlling Food Hazards**   Page 4

    This section applies to ALL food businesses.

2. **General Requirements for Food Premises**   Page 8

    This section applies to ALL food premises except mobile and/or temporary premises, premises used occasionally for commercial food preparation, vending machines and domestic premises.

3. **Specific Requirements for Rooms Where Food is Prepared, Processed**   Page 15
    or Treated

    This section applies to ALL food premises except mobile and/or temporary premises, premises used occasionally for commerical food preparation, vending machines and domestic premises. Examples of processing operation might include filleting fish, dicing meats, crab boiling, making sandwiches or vegetable preparation.

    N.B. You will also need to comply with the 'General Requirements for Food Premises'.

4. **Mobile and Temporary Premises**   Page 20

    This section applies to ALL food businesses which operate from temporary/mobile premises and stalls, including handcarts.

5. **Transport**   Page 30

    This section applies to ALL food businesses.

This section applies to ALL food businesses.

Legal Requirement

Regulation 4(3) of the Regulations states that *"A proprietor of a food business shall identify any step in the activities of the food business which is critical to ensuring food safety and ensure that adequate safety procedures are identified, implemented, maintained and reviewed on the basis of the following principles -*

(a)   *analysis of the potential food hazards in a food business operation;*

(b)   *identification of the points in those operations where food hazards may occur;*

(c)   *deciding which of the points identified are critical to ensuring food safety ("critical points");*

(d)   *identification and implementation of effective control and monitoring procedures at those critical points; and*

(e)   *review of the analysis of food hazards, the critical points and the control and monitoring procedures periodically, and whenever the food business's operations change".*

Objective of the Regulation

This Regulation is a new legal requirement and it places a responsibility on the proprietor to identify and assess food safety risks associated with a particular business or operation. Every food business must apply the principles to their own particular situation.

The Regulation is based on a system of identification and control of **'food hazards'**. A food hazard is anything which may cause harm to someone eating the food. This includes existing contamination and accidental or deliberate contamination by:

- chemicals (e.g. cleaning materials or pest baits);
- bacteria and other micro-organisms which cause food poisoning (e.g. Salmonella, E.coli);
- foreign objects (e.g. jewellery, hair, glass, metal).

The identification of food hazards, the steps at which they could occur and the introduction of measures to control them is called **'hazard analysis'**. Although hazard analysis may seem a complicated process, it is relatively straight forward if carried out step by step.

A hazard analysis must place particular emphasis on virulent food poisoning organisms such as E.coli 0157.

The approach is based on the five principles (a) to (e) above, which are dealt with individually in the following tables.

Legal requirement	Guide to compliance

4(3)(a)
analysis of the potential food hazards in a food business operation;

Every proprietor must identify the possible hazards in their own business (e.g. chemical, bacterial or foreign objects).

4(3)(b)
identification of the points in those operations where food hazards may occur;

Identify <u>all</u> the stages involved in your business and the types of food handled, from receipt of the food to selling to the consumer. Stages include delivery, storage, handling, preparation, cooking, display, service, wrapping.

Hazards can occur at any one or more of the steps. The possible hazards at each stage must be identified. Examples include:

- Multiplication of food poisoning bacteria to harmful levels due to storage/display of 'high risk food' (see definition, page 140) at incorrect temperatures.

- Passage of bacteria from hands onto food due to staff not washing hands before handling open food.

- Foreign objects such as glass, metal or plastic gaining access to food during wrapping, portioning or service of food.

- Contamination by pests such as mice, flying insects, birds or cockroaches during delivery, storage, handling, cooking, display, service or wrapping.

- Deliberate or inadvertent contamination of food at any stage of the process.

4(3)(c)
deciding which of the points identified are critical to ensuring food safety ('critical points');

'Critical points' are steps at which the food hazards must be controlled to ensure that they are eliminated or reduced to a safe level.

A decision must be made as to whether the potential hazard you have identified at each stage needs to be controlled at that point to ensure the safety of the food for the consumer; if it does, then that stage is a 'critical control point'.

Examples include:

- raw meat may contain food poisoning bacteria but cooking correctly will reduce the hazard. Thus the purchase and storage of raw meat is not a critical point with regard to bacterial contamination, but the subsequent stage of cooking is a critical control point.

- Both the storage and the display of ready to eat food such as cooked meats are critical points in terms of controlling contamination by, and the growth of, bacteria, as these foods will receive no further treatment to eliminate/reduce the hazard before consumption.

Legal requirement	Guide to compliance

4(3)(d)
identification and implementation of effective control and monitoring procedures at those critical points; and

Identify what action you have to take to reduce the food hazards at these critical points, implement the action and monitor it to ensure it is effective. The action which it is necessary to take is a 'control measure'. Examples of control measures include:

- Effective stock control and rotation to ensure that all food is sold within its 'use by' date.
- Joints of meat, chicken and reformed meats, such as beefburgers, must be cooked thoroughly to kill any food poisoning bacteria. It is useful to use a temperature probe to check that they have been heated to at least 75°C in their thickest part.
- Display ready to eat cooked meats at a temperature of 8°C or below to help reduce the growth of some food poisoning bacteria. Regularly check the temperature at which your display cabinet is operating (5°C will allow a margin of error below the legal standard in England and Wales).
- Separate raw and cooked foods within display cabinets to prevent cross contamination. Regularly check that separation is adequate.
- Make staff aware of the standards of personal hygiene to be observed (see page 39) and check to ensure that they are complying.

If the control measure is based on cooking at a particular temperature for a particular time, ensure that both temperature and time are monitored.

Keep premises and equipment clean.

4(3)(e)
review of the analysis of food hazards, the critical points and the control and monitoring procedures periodically, and whenever the food business's operations change.

The hazard analysis system must be reviewed on a regular basis (e.g. every year) and be kept up to date to take account of any changes to your food business. Such changes could include altering the range of food you sell, changing supplier or staff or installing new display/refrigeration/cooking equipment. When changes do occur, you must go through the steps (a) to (d) above to identify controls and monitor critical points.

RECOMMENDATIONS OF GOOD PRACTICE

(Not a Legal Requirement)

This Regulation does not demand fully documented hazard analysis systems. However, a brief written explanation of the food hazards, with critical points identified, and control measures and monitoring methods used, together with monitoring records, will help to show enforcement officers that this Regulation has been complied with. It may also help to provide evidence for a defence of `due diligence' should a prosecution be brought against you.

Summary

1. Look at all stages of your operation.

2. Identify any hazards at each stage.

3. Decide at which stage the hazard must be controlled.

4. Implement the controls and monitor them.

5. Review the process periodically.

An example of this process for various food businesses is included in each of the traders' checklists in Part 5.

A blank table is included as Appendix A which may be photocopied for your use.

Reference may also be made to the Department of Health booklet `A Guide to food hazards and your business' which is freely available from your local Environmental Health Department or from Department of Health, PO Box 410, Wetherby, LS23 7LN.

Part 3   SCHEDULE 1
THE 'RULES OF HYGIENE'

Chapter I   General Requirements for Food Premises
(Other than Temporary or Mobile)

Food Premises are any premises or areas of premises in which food or drink is prepared, served or stored. This chapter applies to permanent stalls (see Glossary, page 140) and storage areas.

Legal requirement	Guide to compliance	Advice on good practice
1. Food premises must be kept clean and maintained in good repair and condition.	All parts of the food premises (floors, walls, ceilings, light fittings, ventilation systems, fixed equipment, sinks, wash hand basins, and toilets) must be visually clean and in a good state of repair. **What to clean and/or disinfect:** i) Floors, walls and ceiling areas must be thoroughly cleaned and degreased. ii) Walls immediately behind food preparation surfaces and equipment used for high risk food must be cleaned and disinfected to reduce the risk of food contamination. iii) Food contact surfaces, cutting boards, slicing machines, utensils and handles of drawers and refrigerators must be cleaned and disinfected, particularly if used for raw food before high risk food is prepared. Cleaning and disinfection will normally require access to a sink. This will usually be on the stall/premises. The use of communal facilities, where available, is acceptable for businesses selling only low risk foods such as: ● pre-wrapped or bottled goods; ● open dried goods such as sweets, nuts, cereals, and plain bread products; ● whole fruit and vegetables. The sink unit must be provided with an adequate supply of hot and cold (or warm) water from a potable supply (drinking water). See Water Supply, Part 3, Chapter VII, page 37. Regular inspection of food premises is essential to identify any structural defects or broken equipment and to arrange for remedial action.	It is strongly advised that there should be routine cleaning schedules to ensure that all parts of the premises, equipment and utensils are thoroughly cleaned, on a regular basis. The cleaning schedule should be in written form and should include the following: ● the area to be cleaned; ● the product used; ● method and standard required; ● the frequency of cleaning; ● any health and safety precautions; ● who cleaned by? ● who checked by? An essential ingredient of any cleaning schedule is for management to ensure that it is carried out regularly, efficiently and effectively. Management should check and countersign the schedule. See Appendix C. Encourage staff to 'clean as they go'. Commercial quality stainless steel sinks with integral upstand and drainer are recommended. It is good practice to avoid business disruptions, due to defective or broken equipment (especially through many items failing in a short time period), by planned maintenance and replacement programmes for premises and equipment. Time intervals for maintenance and replacement should be based on the quality of materials, construction and the likely usage/wear. Premises and equipment should be in good repair and condition, efficient working order, safe and capable of being cleaned.

Legal requirement	Guide to compliance	Advice on good practice
2. The layout, design, construction and size of food premises shall-		
(a) permit adequate cleaning and/or disinfection;	The layout and design of food premises must allow access for cleaning to all parts of the premises.

The construction, structure and surface finishes within food premises determines how easily they can be cleaned. | Island siting of equipment is recommended. |
	It is essential that the correct materials are chosen for all ceiling, wall and floor finishes and that they are properly fixed or applied. See Appendix E for further details.	The junction between the walls and the floor should be coved where possible to facilitate cleaning.
(b) be such as to protect against the accumulation of dirt,	Voids/dead areas between the structure, work surfaces, and equipment; cracks/joints in surface finishes; and long pipework runs are best avoided as these areas will become dirt traps.	
contact with toxic materials,	Construction materials and surface finishes must not include any materials which might add poisonous materials to food.	There should be separate storage facilities/space for cleaning materials and other chemicals away from food. All containers should be suitably labelled.
the shedding of particles into food	Surface finishes which may lead to the shedding of particles (e.g. flaking paint, plaster, or fibres) must be avoided. If this is not possible they must be kept in good condition and repair with regular checks being made.	
and the formation of condensation or undesirable mould on surfaces;	Construction materials and surface finishes must be chosen to prevent and reduce condensation and mould growth.	In areas where steam and humidity are generated, surfaces such as ceilings should be insulated/installed to reduce the formation of condensation droplets. Painted surfaces should contain suitable fungicide to reduce mould growth.

Legal requirement	Guide to compliance	Advice on good practice
(c) permit good food hygiene practices, including protection against cross contamination between and during operations, by foodstuffs, equipment, materials, water, air supply or personnel and external sources of contamination such as pests; and	Most food premises carry out many different activities such as cleaning, storage, preparation and waste disposal. There must be enough space in food premises to allow separation of clean and "dirty" processes and raw and high risk food preparation (e.g. by providing separate work surfaces and designing the work flow through the premises).

Where space is limited the same area and equipment may be used for raw and high risk foods but cleaning and disinfection must occur between these operations.

Equipment details are given on page 33.

Water supply details are given on page 37.

Natural and/or mechanical ventilation must be designed so that contaminated air (e.g. from toilet or refuse stores) is not brought into food rooms.

Facilities must be provided for good personal hygiene, for example for storage of outdoor clothing and for hand washing.

Premises must be designed to prevent the access of pests, such as rats, mice, birds and insects. | Good layout, production flow and working instructions should ensure that the preparation and handling of raw and high risk foods are separated.

Space in a market stall is limited. Staff should be able to carry out their duties safely and without congestion. |
| | | It is advisable, as a preventative measure, to have a specialist pest control survey of your premises. This will provide advice on proofing your premises to prevent pests gaining access. See Part 3, Chapter II,1,(d), page 16, Chapter II,1,(e),page 17, Chapter VI,(3) page 35 and Chapter IX,(3) page 44.

Staff training should include identification of common pests and indications of pest infestations. |
| | Food must not be placed on the floor. | It is recommended that food be placed at a minimum height of 45 cm above ground level. This will be of particular importance where animals such as dogs are allowed access to public areas. |
| *(d) provide, where necessary, suitable temperature conditions for the hygienic processing and storage of products.* | The design and construction of food preparation rooms must be such as to prevent condensation and avoid the build up of excessive temperatures and humidity, which could compromise food safety.

Compliance with the Temperature Regulations is required, see Part 4 , page 52. | |

Food Safety (General Food Hygiene) Regulations 1995 – Guide to compliance for Markets & Fairs

Legal requirement	Guide to compliance	Advice on good practice
3. An adequate number of washbasins must be available, suitably located and designated for cleaning hands.	All food businesses must have access to a wash hand basin. Communal facilities may be used, where available, by food businesses selling low risk products such as: ● pre-wrapped or bottled goods; ● open dried goods such as sweets, nuts, cereals and plain bread products; ● whole fruit and vegetables. Staff working on these stalls/premises must have access to these facilities at all times (e.g. to wash their hands after nose blowing, handling rubbish, cleaning operations). If they are unable to leave the stall to do this (e.g. due to staffing levels) a wash hand basin must be provided on the stall/premises. Alternatively, the use of a single facility on the stall for these businesses, for hand, food and equipment washing, is acceptable, provided that these activities can be carried out effectively and without prejudice to food safety. It may be necessary to clean and disinfect the sink between different uses. Businesses selling open high risk foods must have separate hand washing facilities on the stall. Where there is mains drainage, wash hand basins must have a trapped connection to the foul drainage system. Where there is no mains drainage system, enclosed or covered liquid waste containers must be provided.	Suitable materials for a wash hand basin could include: ● stainless steel; ● food grade plastic; ● ceramic. It is strongly recommended that where any open food is handled on the stall, a wash hand basin is provided at each individual unit rather than relying on communal facilities. Wash hand basins should be conveniently accessible so that staff can **easily** use them without, for example, reaching, stretching, bending or having to move other equipment. Wash hand basins with foot, knee or "automatic operated" taps are recommended where raw and high risk foods are handled. In larger premises, especially where high risk food is handled, additional wash hand basins may be required. See Part 3, Chapter III, 2(f), page 26 for information on how to deal with liquid waste.
An adequate number of flush lavatories must be available and connected to an effective drainage system.	Communal toilet facilities may be used or there may be an individual toilet provided within the premises. Toilets must be provided on the basis of the Workplace (Health, Safety and Welfare) Regulations 1992. The minimum requirement is 1 toilet for up to 5 employees.	Notices requesting users to wash their hands after using the toilet should be fixed in a suitable position near every toilet used by food handlers. It is recommended that staff and public facilities are separate.

Legal requirement	Guide to compliance	Advice on good practice
Lavatories must not lead directly into rooms in which food is handled.	Where a toilet is provided within the food business or stall this must not connect directly into a room where open food is handled or stored. Food must not be stored in the intervening ventilated space between the toilets and food rooms.	The intervening space between the toilets and food rooms should be ventilated. Self closing devices should be fitted to the doors.
4. Wash basins for cleaning hands must be provided with		
hot and cold (or appropriately mixed) running water,	The water supply must be potable (drinking) water. See Water Supply, Part 3, Chapter VII, page 37. Where services are readily available, a separate hot and cold water supply or warm water from either a constant piped supply or an instantaneous water heater (gas/electric) is able to be provided to the wash hand basin. If services are not available at the premises/stall, insulated containers for hot water storage would be acceptable, provided they are of a suitable capacity and are capable of storing the water at an adequate temperature. A separate container of cold water may also be required. It is recommended that stalls selling open high risk foods have the water from the containers piped to the wash hand basin.	See Part 3, Chapter III, 2(e), page 25, for information on providing potable water other than directly from a mains supply.
materials for cleaning hands	A supply of soap or detergent must be provided for cleaning hands.	It is good practice to use a bactericidal liquid soap from a wall mounted dispenser.
and for hygienic drying.	Drying facilities can include: ● disposable paper towels; ● roller paper cabinet towels; ● washable fabric roller towels in cabinets; ● warm air dryers.	Disposable paper towels (with provision for the storage of used towels) are recommended. Air dryers are useful when the time available for drying hands is not limited.

Food Safety (General Food Hygiene) Regulations 1995 – Guide to compliance for Markets & Fairs

Legal requirement	Guide to compliance	Advice on good practice
Where necessary, the provision for washing food must be separate from the hand washing facility.	Where food is washed on the stall and open high risk food is handled, the hand washing facilities must be separate from any facilities provided for food washing.	It is good practice to have signs to identify designated 'hand wash' basins.
5. There must be suitable and sufficient means of natural or mechanical ventilation.	Natural or mechanical ventilation must be provided to ensure that heat or humidity do not build up to levels that could compromise food safety, and to avoid condensation. It is recommended that this is in the form of a canopy, connected to a flue with a mechanical extract fan, filters and grease trap, above any cooking or frying range.	As a target, ambient temperatures should be below 25°C. Reliance upon natural ventilation/market hall ventilation system is likely to be satisfactory for most small scale retail operations. Ventilation canopies should extend over cooking equipment by at least 230 mm. Metal canopies are best constructed of stainless or galvanised steel and should incorporate a cleanable channel around the lower edge to collect condensation.
Mechanical air flow from a contaminated area to a clean area must be avoided.	Mechanical ventilation must be designed to avoid air flow from a "dirty" area (e.g. waste storage areas, toilets, pot washing areas) to "clean" areas (e.g. serveries, displays, preparation areas). Air intake into the premises must be placed away from drainage fresh air inlets and stack ventilation pipes.	
Ventilation systems must be so constructed as to enable filters and other parts requiring cleaning or replacement to be readily accessible.	Access to filters, ducting and fans (e.g. through maintenance hatches) is essential to permit routine cleaning and maintenance.	Spare sets of either washable or disposable filters should be kept for cleaning and replacement purposes. Ducting with spans over 2 metres or changes in direction should have inspection or cleaning panels fitted at convenient intervals to allow access for cleaning.
6. All sanitary conveniences within food premises shall be provided with adequate natural or mechanical ventilation.	Toilet accommodation must have either natural or mechanical ventilation to prevent aerosols and offensive odours penetrating food rooms.	Where ventilation is by mechanical means, extract ventilation should be provided to produce a minimum of 3, and preferably 6, air changes per hour.
7. Food premises must have adequate natural and/or artificial lighting.	Natural or artificial lighting must be available to all parts of the food premises and must be good enough to facilitate safe food handling, cleaning and inspection.	Recommended illumination levels vary from 150 lux in store rooms to 500 lux in food preparation areas.

Legal requirement	Guide to compliance	Advice on good practice
		Where open food is handled, lights should be enclosed to prevent contamination of food in the event of damage to the fitting, and to facilitate cleaning. For example fluorescent light fittings should either be provided with diffusers or be fitted with protected tubes.
		Light fittings should be flush mounted where possible and not suspended on hanging chains as these are dirt traps.
		Where practicable, wiring should be chased into the walls or ceiling. The use of surface mounted conduits and surface mounted switch boxes should be avoided.
8. Drainage facilities must be adequate for the purpose intended; they must be designed and constructed to avoid the risk of contamination of foodstuffs.	Drains must be of sufficient size and fall to allow efficient disposal of waste water and soil drainage and prevent entry of foul air from the drainage system into any food room.	Regular maintenance and good housekeeping practices are recommended to prevent excessive discharges of fat, oil, or grease entering the system.
	All feed into drains must pass through an effective trap.	
	Fresh air inlets and stack ventilation pipes must not be situated in a food room and must be placed away from any air intake into the premises.	
	It is recommended that internal inspection chambers be avoided wherever possible. Where unavoidable they must be provided with secured, sealed, air tight double covers. They must also be accessible for maintenance (i.e. avoid building cupboards or other fixed structures over them).	
9. Adequate changing facilities for personnel must be provided where necessary.	A changing facility or area away from where open high risk food is handled must be provided where staff have to change out of outdoor, or contaminated, clothing into protective clothing. Communal facilities are acceptable.	Suitable lockers for the storage of outdoor clothing and personal effects should be provided. Also small lockers on individual stalls for valuable personal effects may be useful.

Food Safety (General Food Hygiene) Regulations 1995 – Guide to compliance for Markets & Fairs

SCHEDULE 1
             THE 'RULES OF HYGIENE'

Chapter II   **Specific Requirements Where Foodstuffs Are Prepared, Treated Or Processed (Excluding Temporary And/Or Mobile Premises)**

This chapter only applies to stalls/rooms in which food or drink is prepared, treated and processed. It therefore includes permanent stalls (see Glossary, page 140) and premises preparing, cutting, cooking or packing food, but not food storage rooms.

Legal requirement	Guide to compliance	Advice on good practice
1. In rooms where food is prepared, treated or processed (excluding dining areas) -		
(a) floor surfaces must be maintained in a sound condition and they must be easy to clean and, where necessary, disinfect.	Floors must be kept in a good state of repair which allows them to be kept clean and capable of being disinfected.	It is strongly advised that there should be routine cleaning schedules to ensure that all parts of the premises, equipment, and utensils are thoroughly cleaned on a regular basis. See Appendix C.
This will require the use of impervious, non-absorbent, washable and non toxic materials, unless the proprietor of the food business can satisfy the food authority that other materials used are appropriate.	A range of options for flooring materials exists dependent upon the type of food business or the particular area of operation. See Appendix E for further details.	Where tiles are used, joints between tiles should be kept to a minimum, both in size and number, so that they are easier to keep clean.
Where appropriate, floors must allow adequate surface drainage;	Where there is likely to be significant spillage or wet cleaning methods are used, floor drains will be required, unless other methods of removing liquids are used, (e.g. wet vacuuming).	Where floor drains are present, floors should "fall" towards the floor drain to avoid ponding. A minimum fall of 1 in 60 is recommended. Drains should be trapped and floor drains kept clean.
(b) wall surfaces must be maintained in a sound condition and they must be easy to clean and, where necessary, disinfect.	Walls must be kept in good repair to allow effective cleaning. Areas immediately behind food preparation surfaces and equipment must be capable of being cleaned and disinfected to reduce the risk of food contamination.	Walls which are light coloured will assist in monitoring cleaning. They should be free of ledges/projections/ornamentation. Proprietary wall sheeting and systems should be designed for food use and properly installed.
This will require the use of impervious, non-absorbent, washable and non-toxic materials and require a smooth surface up to a height appropriate for the operations, unless the proprietor of the food business can satisfy the food authority that other materials used are appropriate;	A range of options for wall finishes exists dependent upon the type of food business or the particular area of operation. See Appendix E for further details.	Walls behind equipment such as sinks, cookers, work surfaces and wash hand basins usually require higher durability finishes. For example tiled splashbacks or stainless steel, to an appropriate height and width that will accommodate splashing and damage.
		Areas close to heat sources should be capable of withstanding the temperatures they are subjected to.
		A smooth, washable surface is recommended to a height of at least 1.8m above floor level.

Legal requirement	Guide to compliance	Advice on good practice
(c) ceilings and overhead fixtures must be designed, constructed and finished to prevent the accumulation of dirt and reduce condensation, the growth of undesirable moulds and the shedding of particles;	The roof of the market hall or the ceilings to individual stalls must be constructed and designed to: ● allow periodic cleaning; ● reduce condensation and mould growth; ● prevent the shedding of particles (e.g. flaking paint, plaster, or fibres). A range of options exists for ceiling finishes dependent upon the type of food business and the particular area of operation. See Appendix E for further details.	Surface finishes should be light coloured to assist in monitoring cleaning. Light fittings should be flush mounted and not suspended on hanging chains as these are dirt traps. In areas where steam and humidity are generated ceilings should be insulated to prevent the formation of condensation droplets and painted surfaces should contain a suitable fungicide to reduce mould growth. Ceilings should be kept in good condition and repair with regular checks being made to prevent the shedding of particles. Junctions between ceilings and walls should be coved to facilitate cleaning.
(d) windows and other openings must be constructed to prevent the accumulation of dirt. Those which can be opened to the outside environment must where necessary be fitted with insect-proof screens which can be easily removed for cleaning. Where open windows would result in contamination of foodstuffs, windows must remain closed and fixed during production;	Windows and other openings must be constructed to provide a surface which can be kept clean. Suitable options for windows are: ● simple design anodised aluminium or UPVC window frame; ● simple design timber window frames of good quality smooth planed timber, decorated to a smooth, washable finish (e.g. gloss paint). Windows must be screened if: ● they open directly into food preparation areas **and** ● they are opened for ventilation during food preparation **and** ● screening is necessary to prevent a risk of infestation and/or contamination. Where dirt build-up on insect proof screens may present a risk of food contamination, the screens must be designed to be easily removed for cleaning.	Window rebates and sills should be finished to the same standards as the walls. Sloping window sills help to prevent accumulation of dirt. A light coloured surface finish is recommended to assist in monitoring cleaning.

Legal requirement	Guide to compliance	Advice on good practice
(e) doors must be easy to clean and, where necessary, disinfect. This will require the use of smooth and non-absorbent surfaces, unless the proprietor of the food business can satisfy the food authority that other materials used are appropriate;	Provide doors with surfaces which can be kept clean and which allow effective and easy cleaning. Any door used by staff who handle open food, where they are likely to touch the door and door furniture, must be capable of being disinfected. Suitable options for doors are: ● solid construction flush design doors; ● sealed hollow section flush design doors finished in a smooth, washable coating of sufficient durability (e.g. wood, metal, rubber, PVC or safety glass); ● timber frame - good quality timber, smooth planed finish, properly decorated to a smooth, washable finish; ● UPVC or anodised aluminium doors and frames.	Door frames should be effectively sealed to the wall and floor finish material and architrave should be avoided to limit unnecessary voids. Door furniture should be of plain design to facilitate cleaning. "Kick-plates" and "rubbing strips" improve the durability of the door finish. External doors and frames should be rodent proof (e.g. the bottom gap between the door and the threshold should be kept very close or effective bristle or rubber stripping provided). Light coloured surface finishes are recommended to assist in monitoring cleaning. External door openings may need to be fitted with self-closing, washable mesh insect screens where the doors are left open for any length of time and pest entry to food handling areas is likely. The screens should be capable of being removed for effective cleaning. External doors and doors to lobbies should be self-closing.
(f) surfaces (including surfaces of equipment) in contact with food must be maintained in a sound condition and be easy to clean and, where necessary, disinfect. This will require the use of smooth, washable and non-toxic materials, unless the proprietor of the food business can satisfy the food authority that other materials used are appropriate.	Food preparation surfaces, work tops, and equipment that come into contact with food must be easy to clean and maintained in a sound condition. This will involve regular inspection to identify any defects with the necessary remedial action being taken. This may include inspection of any communal facilities by the market or fair operator. They must be capable of being disinfected regularly and between use for raw and high risk food preparation. Surfaces which comply include: ● stainless steel; ● ceramic; ● food grade plastics. See Chapter V, Equipment Requirements, page 33, for further guidance, including the use of wooden chopping blocks.	

Legal requirement	Guide to compliance	Advice on good practice
2. *Where necessary, adequate facilities must be provided for the cleaning and disinfecting of work tools and equipment. These facilities must be constructed of materials resistant to corrosion and must be easy to clean and have an adequate supply of hot and cold water.*	All food businesses must have access to facilities (e.g. sinks and dishwashers) for the cleaning of premises and equipment. The size of sink needed will relate to the proposed use or size of equipment to be washed. Where services are readily available, a separate hot and cold potable (drinking) water supply, or warm water from either a constant piped supply or an instantaneous water heater (gas/electric), is able to be provided to the sink. If services are not available at the premises/stall, insulated containers for hot water storage are acceptable provided they are of a suitable capacity and are capable of storing the water at an adequate temperature. A separate container of cold potable water may also be required. It is recommended that, for stalls selling open high risk foods, water from the containers is piped to the sink. See also Chapter I, pages 8 and 11.	Commercial quality stainless steel sinks with integral upstands and drainers are recommended. Where there is a junction between the sink and wall, cleaning at the junction should be facilitated by either: ● providing a flush fixing with overtiling; ● setting upstand 150 mm clear of wall surface; ● providing mobile sinks with flexible couplings. Communal sinks could be used for cleaning equipment such as mops and buckets. Such sinks should be designated as solely for this use.
3. *Where appropriate, adequate provision must be made for any necessary washing of the food. Every sink or other such facility provided for the washing of food must have an adequate supply of hot and/or cold potable water as required, and be kept clean.*	In most small retail or catering operations one sink is acceptable for both equipment and food washing, provided that both activities can be carried out effectively and without prejudice to food safety. It may be necessary to clean and disinfect the sink between different uses. Separate sinks for equipment washing and food preparation must be provided, where there is a greater volume of preparation work, and equipment washing and food washing; or where it is impractical to clean and disinfect a single facility between uses. Where services are readily available, a separate supply of hot and cold potable (drinking) water, or warm water from either a constant piped supply or an instantaneous water heater (gas/electric), is able to be provided to the sink.	Some of the bacteria which cause food poisoning may survive in soil and can, therefore, contaminate root vegetables. It is recommended that any sink used to clean vegetables is cleaned and disinfected after use. In larger catering premises separate sinks are recommended for vegetables, salads, meat and fish. It is good practice to have signs above sinks indicating what they can be used for, (e.g. "Food Only", "Equipment Only").

If services are not available at the premises/stall, insulated containers for hot water storage are acceptable, provided they are of a suitable capacity and are capable of storing the water at an adequate temperature.

A separate container of cold potable water may also be required.

It is recommended that for stalls selling open high risk foods, the water from the containers is piped to the sink.

Hot water supply is not essential if a sink is to be used exclusively for the preparation of a single food type (e.g. washing salads only).

Hot water will still need to be provided if the sink is used to prepare different types of food, (e.g. raw chicken and salad) and therefore needs to be cleaned and/or disinfected between uses. See also Chapter I, pages 11-13.

Part 3   SCHEDULE 1
          THE 'RULES OF HYGIENE'

Chapter III   Mobile And Temporary Premises

This section applies to temporary stalls (see Glossary, page 141), both indoor and outdoor, and handcarts at markets, fairs and shows. It also applies to mobile vehicles and street traders. Tents and marquees, used for catering purposes at larger outdoor events, are covered by both the "Catering Guide to Good Hygiene Practice" and this Guide, and you may refer to either Guide for guidance on compliance with the Regulations and Temperature Regulations.

This Guide has not attempted to give guidance on vending machines or domestic premises which are seen as outside the scope of markets and fairs.

The legal requirements for mobile and temporary premises focus more on practices than structural measures and equipment provision, to reflect the practical considerations.

Legal requirement	Guide to compliance	Advice on good practice
1. Premises and vending machines shall be so sited, designed, constructed, and kept clean and maintained in good repair and condition, so as to avoid the risk of contaminating foodstuffs and harbouring pests, so far as is reasonably practicable.	**Siting** Stalls, vehicles and handcarts must be away from sources of contamination such as refuse stores, smoking bonfires, toilets, ditches or open drains and areas that could flood, where the food could not be adequately protected. **Design and Construction** The stall, vehicle or handcart must be large enough for the type of operation carried on (e.g. sufficient working surfaces for the separate preparation of raw and cooked products) so that cross contamination cannot occur, unless those surfaces are disinfected between uses. Where possible, the design of mobile and temporary premises should avoid the risk of harbouring pests. Where this is not practical then the food itself must be protected from contamination by pests e.g. by covering or wrapping. All internal surfaces must be constructed of washable materials. See Appendix E for acceptable finishes for mobile and temporary premises.	On sites used regularly for markets and fairs, it is good practice to locate mobile and temporary stalls and handcarts on a suitable hard standing and near to key services such as water, drainage and electricity. Businesses should liaise with the market or fair operator to minimise any problems with the siting of their stall. For "one off" events advance preparation, discussion and site meetings should be conducted to consider the type of food businesses which will be present, the facilities required, and the best operational layout.

The type of floor finish used will depend on the nature of the site and food handled. The following types of floor construction and finish are considered suitable for sites on grass or earth, where there is no open high risk food:

- substantial sealed wooden duck board;
- synthetic duck board;
- concrete slabs on sand.

Duck boards must be kept in good repair in order to enable them to be kept clean.

Since duckboards do not provide a continuous washable surface, food etc. may accumulate, and contamination may penetrate from underneath. Working practices should reflect this.

Where there is open high risk food:

- cleanable sheeting material should be provided under washable duck boarding to facilitate removal of any spillages and prevent ingress of grass between the slats;
- slabs should be closely abutted and sealed so they are non-porous and washable.

If open food is to be sold from a stall or hand cart it must be protected from contamination. This may be achieved by the provision of a stall cover (top, back, and sides) or through the construction of the unit itself.

Natural or mechanical ventilation will be required so that internal temperatures and humidity do not compromise food safety.

Reliance upon natural ventilation/existing ventilation systems is likely to be satisfactory for most small scale retail operations.

Adequate artificial lighting must be provided when necessary.

Artificial lighting needs may be greater in winter.

Cleanliness, Maintenance and Repair
The stall, vehicle or handcart must be maintained in a good state of repair, to enable effective cleaning to be carried out and avoid contamination of food (e.g. surfaces kept free from cracks, splits, chips or flaking decoration).

Regular inspection is essential to identify any structural defects or broken equipment and to arrange for remedial action.
Provision needs to be made for stalls or vehicles which are only used occasionally or seasonally (i.e. checking and remedial cleaning or repair prior to use after periods of non use/storage).

A greater frequency and depth of cleaning will be required where open high risk foods are handled.
Where possible, stalls should be dismantled if this allows more effective cleaning.

The stall/vehicle/hand cart must be cleaned down prior to handling foods and regularly thereafter to remove visible dirt and debris.

More information about cleaning schedules can be found in Appendix C.

Surfaces which come into contact with open high risk food must be disinfected prior to starting work and between uses when both raw and cooked food is handled.

Legal requirement	Guide to compliance	Advice on good practice

2. In particular and where necessary -

(a) appropriate facilities must be available to maintain adequate personal hygiene (including facilities for the hygienic washing and drying of hands, hygienic sanitary arrangements and changing facilities);

All food businesses must have access to a wash hand basin or bowl for the hygienic cleaning and drying of hands.

The use of communal facilities, where available, is acceptable for businesses selling only low risk foods, such as:
- pre-wrapped, tinned or bottled goods;
- open dried goods such as sweets, nuts, cereals and plain bread products;
- whole fruit and vegetables;

provided that staff have convenient access to these facilities at all times (i.e. to clean their hands after nose blowing, handling rubbish, cleaning operations or performing other operations which may contaminate the hands) and are able to leave the stall, vehicle or handcart.

Alternatively, the use of a single facility on the stall, vehicle or hand cart for hand, food and equipment washing for these businesses is acceptable, provided that these activities can be carried out effectively and without prejudice to food safety. It may be necessary to clean and disinfect the facility between different uses.

Businesses handling open high risk foods must have separate hand washing facilities on the stall/vehicle/handcart.

A supply of soap or detergent and hand drying facilities must be provided for use with any wash hand basin or bowl.

It is recommended that where any open food (including low risk food) is handled on the stall, vehicle or handcart, facilities are provided at each individual unit rather than relying on communal facilities.

Wash hand basins, bowls or other hand cleaning facilities should be conveniently accessible so that staff can easily use them without, for example, reaching, stretching, bending or having to move other equipment. Commercial quality sanitised handwipes may sometimes provide a more practical option of hand cleaning.

It may be necessary to provide more than one wash hand basin depending on the scale of the operation.

Suitable materials for a wash hand basin could include:
- stainless steel;
- food grade plastic;
- ceramic.

It is good practice to provide a bactericidal soap for washing hands, where high risk food is handled. It is recommended that disposable paper towels are the first choice for hand drying. A bin will be required for the disposal of paper towels.

Legal requirement	Guide to compliance	Advice on good practice
	Toilet Facilities Clean, well lit toilets must be available nearby for stalls, vehicles or handcarts. There must be a wash hand basin near to each toilet, provided with soap, a means of drying hands and a supply of potable (drinking) water.	Notices requesting users to wash their hands after using the toilet should be fixed in a suitable position near every toilet used by food handlers. Bactericidal soap and disposable paper towels (with provision for the storage of used towels) for drying hands are recommended. Where these facilities are provided by market operators, it should be made clear who is responsible for cleaning, providing soap and hand drying facilities. See Part 6, Market and Fairs Operators, page 124.
	Changing Facilities Where necessary for preventing food contamination, a space or a separate area away from open food must be provided for staff to change into protective overclothing, (e.g. at show grounds, for changing muddy shoes and coats). Suitable and separate storage facilities must be provided for outdoor clothing and protective clothing for those working in open food areas, where necessary to prevent food contamination.	Suitable storage space should be set aside for outdoor clothing and personal belongings, away from open food on the stall (e.g. locker, cupboard, plastic box or bag). Alternatively, these may be stored in the cab of a mobile vehicle or in a vehicle separate from the stall. Protective overclothing should be protected from contamination in transit (e.g. by keeping it in a plastic wrapper or bag). Food handlers should avoid changing into protective overclothing too far away from the stall when it will be open to contamination en route.
(b) surfaces in contact with food must be in a sound condition and be easy to clean and, where necessary, disinfect. This will require the use of smooth, washable, non-toxic materials, unless the proprietor of the food business can satisfy the food authority that other materials used are appropriate;	Tables, working surfaces, food display cabinets, counters, equipment, utensils and display containers must be in good repair in order to be easy to clean. If open high risk foods touch any surfaces those surfaces must be capable of being disinfected. Regular inspection is essential to ensure that surfaces are in sound condition and to arrange for remedial action. Walls immediately behind and adjacent to food preparation surfaces and equipment must be capable of being cleaned and, in high risk food areas, disinfected.	Joints between work surfaces should be sealed to facilitate effective cleaning and disinfection and to prevent the formation of dirt traps. See Part 3, Chapter V, page 33 for further information on equipment requirements.

Legal requirement	Guide to compliance	Advice on good practice
	Suitable materials for food contact surfaces include: ● stainless steel; ● ceramic; ● food grade plastics.	
	Wooden blocks or unsealed wooden surfaces must not be used for ready to eat foods. Wooden chopping blocks are acceptable for use with raw meat provided they are in good condition and free from cracks and splits.	Correct cleaning of wooden chopping blocks is likely to include scraping to remove surface contamination and cleaning with small amounts of water with a sanitiser.
	Painted/sealed wooden counters or proprietary "plastic grass" may be suitable for whole fruit and vegetables on stalls and handcarts.	
	See Appendix E for examples of acceptable food contact surfaces in mobile and temporary premises.	
(c) adequate provision must be made for the cleaning and, where necessary, disinfecting of work utensils and equipment;	All food businesses will require access to a sink or bowl, usually on the stall/vehicle/handcart, where equipment used on the stall needs to be washed on site to ensure food safety.	Suitable materials for a sink could include: ● stainless steel; ● plastic; ● ceramic.
	Communal facilities may be used, where available, by food businesses selling only low risk food such as: ● pre-wrapped, tinned, or bottled goods; ● open dried foods such as sweets, nuts, cereals, and plain bread products; ● whole fruit and vegetables.	The size of sink needed will relate to the proposed use or size of equipment to be washed. The return of utensils/equipment to base premises for washing up or use of disposable equipment can reduce the level of facilities required. Dirty equipment should be stored so as not to pose a risk of cross contamination to any other food on the stall, vehicle or hand cart. This will only apply where utensils or equipment will not require cleaning between uses whilst out on site (including accidental contamination).
	See also 2(a), page 22 for further details.	
	Food contact surfaces, cutting boards, slicing machines, utensils and handles of drawers and refrigerators will require cleaning and disinfecting if used for raw and high risk food.	Routine cleaning schedules are advisable to ensure that all parts of the premises, equipment and utensils are thoroughly cleaned, on a regular basis. A written cleaning schedule is recommended to include the following: ● the area to be cleaned; ● the product used; ● method and standard required; ● frequency of cleaning; ● any health and safety precautions; ● who cleaned by? ● who checked by? Management should check and countersign the schedule to ensure cleaning is carried out regularly, efficiently and effectively. See Appendix C. Encourage staff to 'clean as they go'.

Legal requirement	Guide to compliance	Advice on good practice
(d) adequate provision must be made for the cleaning of foodstuffs;	In most small retail or catering food businesses where high risk open food is handled, one sink or bowl is acceptable for both equipment and food washing provided that both activities can be carried out effectively and without prejudice to food safety. It may be necessary to clean and disinfect the facility between different uses.	Some of the bacteria which cause food poisoning may survive in soil and can, therefore, contaminate root vegetables. It is recommended that any sink used to clean vegetables is cleaned and disinfected after use.
	Where it is necessary to ensure food safety (e.g. the volume of preparation work demands it), separate facilities for equipment and food washing must be provided.	It is good practice to have signs above sinks indicating what they can be used for, (e.g. "Food Only", "Equipment Only").
	When using communal facilities for washing equipment or food you must ensure there is no risk to food safety. See also 2(a), page 22.	
(e) an adequate supply of hot and/or cold potable water must be available;	All water supplied to hand, equipment and food washing facilities must be potable (drinking) water. See also 2(a) page 22.	
	All food businesses handling high risk open food will require an adequate supply of hot and cold drinking water at the stall, vehicle or handcart.	A minimum of 9 litres of potable (drinking) water is recommended on the stall, vehicle or handcart for hand and equipment washing.
	Food businesses selling only low risk food such as: • pre-wrapped, tinned, or bottled goods; • open dried goods such as sweets, nuts, cereals, and plain bread products; • whole fruit and vegetables; may rely on the use of communal facilities for hand, equipment or food washing, when available. Otherwise, a supply of potable water must be available on the stall, vehicle or handcart.	

Legal requirement	Guide to compliance	Advice on good practice
	Where available, food businesses will be able to use water that comes directly from the mains supply. Otherwise, containers of water may be used which must be filled from a potable water supply (e.g. the mains supply, water tanks/bowsers, or a private water supply).	Advice on the potability of the water supply may be obtained from the market or fair operator, the landowner, or local food authority.
		Filling hoses should be kept clean and all storage tanks should be enclosed or covered.
	Water containers must be kept clean and disinfected frequently to avoid the risk of contamination.	It is good practice to empty water containers and refill with fresh potable water on a daily basis. Water containers and hoses should be disinfected at least weekly.
	Hand and equipment washing facilities must be provided with hot and cold or warm water. Where services are readily available a constant piped supply or an instantaneous water heater (gas/electric) can be used. Alternatively, insulated containers for hot water storage would be acceptable provided they are of suitable capacity and capable of storing the water at an adequate temperature. A separate container of cold water may also be required. It is recommended that for stalls selling open high risk foods, the water from the containers is piped to these facilities.	Clean water containers should not be used for any other purpose and should be clearly distinguishable from containers for waste water.
	A hot water supply is not always essential if a sink is to be used exclusively for food preparation. If it is necessary to ensure food safety, however, (e.g. if different food types are to be washed) then hot water must be provided to facilitate disinfection between uses.	See Part 3, Chapter VII, page 37 and Part 6, Market and Fairs Operators, page 124.
(f) adequate arrangements and/or facilities for the hygienic storage and disposal of hazardous and/or inedible substances and waste (whether liquid or solid) must be available;	Where there is a mains drainage system, waste water from hand, equipment, and food washing facilities can drain into this system via a trapped connection. Otherwise, it must drain into a closed container which must be emptied as required at a suitable disposal point, where there is no risk of food contamination. Where necessary to prevent contamination of food, waste water must not be allowed to drain onto the ground.	Liquid waste containers should be cleaned out at least daily. The waste water should be emptied into the foul drainage system and not, for example, into communal sinks. Containers for "clean" and "waste" water should be easily distinguishable and clearly labelled.
		It is good practice to avoid discharging waste water onto roads as this may enter streams via surface or rain water drainage systems.

Food Safety (General Food Hygiene) Regulations 1995 – Guide to compliance for Markets & Fairs

Legal requirement	Guide to compliance	Advice on good practice
	Refuse and waste must not be allowed to accumulate on the floor. Any waste awaiting removal to central refuse stores must be kept in a suitable container. This must be emptied regularly and not allowed to overflow. The internal and external surfaces of any non-disposable waste container must be washable and in good repair.	Where a bin is provided, plastic linings make removing rubbish and cleaning the bin easier. When rubbish is removed to a central refuse store, the plastic sack should be placed in a lidded, rodent and bird proof container.
	Strong plastic refuse sacks may be used to store waste, provided that they are used in a manner that avoids the contamination of hands or food and the attraction of pests (e.g. regular removal, adequate strength and appropriate location).	Where open food (other than fruit and vegetables) is handled, all bins should have elbow, foot or knee operated lids. Hand operated lids should not be used as these may be a source of contamination.
	For businesses where the only waste produced is dry waste, such as packaging, a closeable container may not be necessary.	
	Cardboard boxes must only be used for dry waste, such as packaging, and must be removed from the food area and disposed of at the end of each day.	
	Waste must not be stored in any way that it will be an attraction to pests.	
	If a central refuse store is not available on site then the container provided must be large enough to hold waste produced during the trading period.	
	The requirements relating to "Central Refuse Stores" are outlined in Part 6, Market and Fair Operators, page 126.	
(g) adequate facilities and/or arrangements for maintaining and monitoring suitable food temperature conditions must be available;	All food that is subject to the Temperature Regulations, is also subject to this section unless exemptions apply. The Temperature Regulations state that in England and Wales, foods which need temperature control for safety must be kept hot (at or above 63°C) or chilled (at or below 8°C). In Scotland, foods which need temperature control for safety must be kept above 63°C or in a refrigerator or cool ventilated place (no temperature specified). See Part 4, Temperature Control, page 52.	Although the Temperature Regulations allow certain relevant foods to be displayed for sale at ambient temperatures, it is good practice to always keep perishable food under a controlled temperature.
	For chilled food it is likely that refrigeration equipment will be needed, although for short periods and for small quantities, an insulated container with eutectic plates/ice packs/ice may be adequate. Insulated containers will only be effective if the food is previously chilled.	The Temperature Regulations relate to the temperature of the food, not the air temperature of the storage area or equipment. It is good practice only to prepare food as it is required, rather than in advance. It is also advisable to reduce the time for which food is out of temperature control to as short a period as possible (e.g. by only bringing it on display as needed to replenish stocks).

Legal requirement	Guide to compliance	Advice on good practice
	For hot food, a hot plate, cabinet or oven will be necessary. Again for very short periods and for small quantities an insulated container may be adequate.	
	Thermometers, or equipment with a temperature display must be available to monitor temperatures.	It is best to make temperature checks at least 3 times per day at appropriate intervals. In addition, a probe thermometer is desirable to check internal food temperatures. The probe should be disinfected before and after each use.
		It is recommended that you keep written records of temperature monitoring. See Appendix B for example recording sheet.
(h) foodstuffs must be so placed as to avoid, so far as is reasonably practicable, the risk of contamination.	The detailed points in Part 3, Chapter IX, 'Provisions Applicable to foodstuffs', page 42, will also apply.	Where possible minimise the amount of food preparation on stalls or mobile vehicles by choosing menus that only require simple cook and serve steps, or by arranging for more elaborate preparation to be completed at a commercial kitchen.
	Likely sources of contamination and examples of protection include:	
	Public - High risk food on display must be protected from the public touching, coughing or sneezing over it. This could involve wrapping, screening or covering the food or placing it out of reach.	
	Animals and Pests - Food must be placed where it cannot be contaminated by animals or pests. This may be by placing food at a suitable height, behind barriers or screens, under covers or in suitable containers, wrappers, storage or display equipment.	It is good practice to ensure pets cannot gain access to food stalls, vehicles, or handcarts by use of appropriate barriers.
	Animals must not be encouraged onto or allowed to stay on stalls, vehicles or handcarts. Measures to discourage pests are outlined in Part 3, Chapter IX, page 44, but not all of these are appropriate on vehicles, temporary stalls and handcarts.	
	Food must not be placed on the ground.	It is recommended that food is placed a minimum height of 45 cm off the ground, particularly where animals such as dogs are allowed access to public areas.
	Natural Elements (i.e. the weather). The stall, vehicle or handcart must be protected from the elements where open food is sold (see notes on design and construction, page 20). Where it is not reasonably practicable to protect food from contamination through the stall, vehicle or handcart design, the food must be otherwise protected by placing it in a suitable position, or container, wrapping, screening or covering.	

Legal requirement	Guide to compliance	Advice on good practice
	Staff - See Personal Hygiene, Part 3, Chapter VIII, page 39.	
	Cross contamination - Raw and cooked foods must be stored and displayed separately, unless they are wrapped so as to prevent cross contamination.	The guidance concerning cross contamination may be updated in the light of specific Government legislative proposals implementing the Pennington Group recommendations for the control of E.coli 0157.
	Food must not be placed in contact with surfaces likely to cause contamination. Food work surfaces and equipment such as tongs, scales and chopping boards must be washed and disinfected before use and between use for raw and cooked foods. Food must not be placed in contact with toxic, flaking or splintering surfaces.	Lidded plastic containers should be used for foods which may drip or leak juices (e.g. meat, fish or liquids). These should be deep enough to contain any juices or other liquids and the food itself. Plastic wrap may be used for bread, pies and other foods not likely to drip.
	Food must be placed so as to avoid risk of contamination by waste, unfit food, raw food, or any drips or leaks from these.	It is good practice to use separate equipment and surfaces for raw and cooked foods where possible, especially if there is limited time for cleaning between uses.

Part 3   SCHEDULE 1
              THE 'RULES OF HYGIENE'

Chapter IV   Transport

This section will apply if you deliver food from wholesalers, cash and carry premises, warehouses, etc. or if you transfer food between your stalls, vehicles, handcarts or premises. This chapter will apply in addition to other parts of the Regulations and the Temperature Regulations.

Legal requirement	Guide to compliance	Advice on good practice
1. Conveyances and/or containers used for transporting foodstuffs must be kept clean and maintained in good repair and condition in order to protect foodstuffs from contamination, and must, where necessary, be designed and constructed to permit adequate cleaning and/or disinfection.	Vehicles and containers (including trolleys, boxes, trays, pallets) used for transporting food must be: ● kept clean; ● made of materials that can be cleaned and disinfected, or disposable (single use) materials, that will not contaminate food; ● kept in good repair.	Vehicles and/or containers should be included in a comprehensive cleaning schedule or have their own individually written schedule. See Appendix C. A designated vehicle or container cleaning area and/or facilities is recommended, (e.g. designated sink and cleaning equipment or separate hose). Vehicles used to transport open high risk foods or raw meat/fish, should be provided with a durable and washable lining which is capable of being disinfected, (e.g. "armadillo" type shell or lining). Ideally, any vehicle used for transporting food should, as far as is practicable, be used solely for that purpose.
2. (1) Receptacles in vehicles and/or containers must not be used for transporting anything other than foodstuffs where this may result in contamination of foodstuffs.	Receptacles must not be used for any other purpose, where subsequent use for transporting food may result in a risk of contaminating that food, or where that use makes it difficult to effectively clean the receptacles.	It is recommended that containers are labelled to indicate their contents in order to assist in preventing contamination.
(2) Bulk foodstuffs in liquid, granulate or powder form must be transported in receptacles and/or containers/tankers reserved for the transport of foodstuffs if otherwise there is a risk of contamination. Such containers must be marked in a clearly visible and indelible fashion, in one or more Community languages, to show that they are used for the transport of foodstuffs, or must be marked "for foodstuffs only".	The bulk transport of food is outside the scope of this Guide.	

Legal requirement	Guide to compliance	Advice on good practice
3. Where conveyances and/or containers are used for transporting anything in addition to foodstuffs or for transporting different foodstuffs at the same time, there must be effective separation of products, where necessary, to protect against the risk of contamination.	If you transport non food items (e.g. refuse, cleaning materials or pet foods) there must be adequate separation to prevent possible contamination of food. If both raw and cooked foods are transported at the same time, the items must be wrapped or kept in separate containers and placed so that no cross contamination can occur. The provisions of Part 3, Chapter IX (3), page 43 will also apply with regard to protecting food against contamination.	As far as practicable, any vehicle used for transporting food, should be reserved solely for that purpose. Alternatively, separate compartments and/or designated containers could be used. Where it is necessary for persons to sleep on the vehicle, the sleeping area/compartment should be physically separated from any food storage or preparation area where possible.
4. Where conveyances and/or containers have been used for transporting anything other than foodstuffs or for transporting different foodstuffs, there must be effective cleaning between loads to avoid the risk of contamination.	Vehicles, containers, trolleys, pallets, or any other conveyances or containers used for transporting different foods, must be cleaned between uses. Containers used for transporting food with a high bacterial load, (e.g. raw meat or raw vegetables) must be cleaned and disinfected before they can be used for ready to eat food.	It is strongly advised that any conveyances and/or containers have their own cleaning schedule or are included as part of a more comprehensive schedule. See Appendix C.
5. Foodstuffs in conveyances and/or containers must be so placed and protected as to minimise the risk of contamination.	Where there is any risk of contamination, food, especially high risk food, must be covered, wrapped and/or placed in sealed, washable containers.	Food grade plastic/stainless steel receptacles are recommended for storage of high risk food during transit.
6. Where necessary, conveyances and/or containers used for transporting foodstuffs, must be capable of maintaining foodstuffs at appropriate temperatures and, where necessary, designed to allow those temperatures to be monitored.	Temperatures at which food must be kept relate to the actual food itself. There are a number of ways to maintain temperatures, depending on the type of vehicle or container and the length of journey. For example: ● insulated boxes containing frozen ice packs may be adequate for transporting chilled food for short local journeys, e.g. less than 2 hours; ● refrigeration equipment to cool the vehicle or container may be necessary for longer journeys or where there are many drop offs. Under the Quick Frozen Foodstuffs Regulations 1990, products labelled 'Quick Frozen' must be kept between -15°C and -18°C.	See Part 4, Temperature Control, page 52. Allowances should be made for traffic problems which may delay local journeys. Frozen food should be kept in its frozen state and not be allowed to defrost, unless it is to be sold unfrozen or immediately processed at the final delivery point. Defrosted food should not be re-frozen and should be labelled 'previously frozen' where necessary.

Part 3

31

Legal requirement	Guide to compliance	Advice on good practice
	If the temperature of the food is a "critical control" then monitoring is required. This could involve probing the food with a thermometer, taking a "between pack" temperature, checking read-outs from vehicles or containers or checking air temperatures of vehicles or containers. It is important to remember that the relevant temperatures refer to the temperature of the food, not the ambient air temperature in the vehicle. Where air temperatures are monitored, it is important to establish the relationship between this temperature and the temperature of the food.	Some vehicles have temperature monitoring equipment which is integral to the vehicle and automatically records the temperature. Where the temperature is taken manually, it is recommended that written records of temperature readings are kept for future reference and that this forms part of your hazard analysis system. See Appendix B.

SCHEDULE 1
THE 'RULES OF HYGIENE'

Chapter V   Equipment Requirements

This section applies to ALL food businesses.

Legal requirement	Guide to compliance	Advice on good practice
1. All articles, fittings and equipment with which food comes into contact shall be kept clean and - *(a) be so constructed, be of such materials, and be kept in such good order, repair and condition, as to minimize any risk of contamination of the food;*	This will relate to any surface that may come into contact with food either directly or in such close proximity that it could contaminate the food if dirty. Examples of such surfaces are: work surfaces, food processing equipment, chopping boards, utensils, crockery, cutlery and glassware. All such surfaces must be kept clean. Suitable materials for work surfaces, equipment, chopping boards and utensils are: ● stainless steel; ● food grade plastics and laminates; ● aluminium and tinned copper (acceptable but less durable). Wooden chopping blocks are acceptable for use with raw meat, provided they are in good condition and free from cracks and splits and kept clean. Wooden blocks or unsealed wooden surfaces must not be used for ready to eat foods.	Equipment should be included as part of a written cleaning schedule or rota to ensure regular cleaning. See Appendix C. When equipment comes into contact with high risk food the cleaning process should include disinfection. The practice of using colour coded synthetic cutting boards and knives is recommended. Correct cleaning of wooden chopping blocks is likely to include scraping to remove surface contamination and cleaning with small amounts of water with a sanitiser.
(b) with the exception of non returnable containers and packaging, be so constructed, be of such materials, and be kept in such good order, repair and condition, as to enable them to be kept thoroughly cleaned and, where necessary, disinfected, sufficient for the purposes intended;	Food equipment, work surfaces, and fittings must be designed with surfaces that allow effective cleaning/disinfection. This is likely to require smooth, impervious finishes. Regular inspection of the above items is necessary to identify any defects (e.g. cracking, splitting, scoring, rusting) which might lead to foreign body contamination, any other form of contamination, or prevent effective cleaning. Once identified, such items must not be used until they have been repaired or replaced.	Design should avoid "dirt traps" (e.g. sharp angles, ledges, open joints). Regular inspections should form part of a planned inspection and maintenance programme.

Legal requirement	Guide to compliance	Advice on good practice
	Food contact surfaces including cutting boards, slicing machines and utensils must be cleaned and disinfected between uses when used for both raw and high risk food preparation.	Equipment should be designed to allow easy dismantling that provides access to all parts that need cleaning. Staff carrying out such cleaning operations should have adequate instruction, supervision and/or training to ensure that they perform this task safely and effectively. See Part 3, Chapter X, page 46.
	Cardboard/waxed paper or similar disposable containers used for food transport/display cannot be effectively cleaned or disinfected and must therefore not be re-used where there is a risk of contamination from subsequent use.	
(c) be installed in such a manner as to allow adequate cleaning of the surrounding area.	Food equipment, work surfaces, and fittings must be installed so that they allow access for cleaning or they must be capable of being moved or dismantled to allow such access. Access is required to clean the appliance itself and the adjoining wall, floor and ceiling surfaces.	Island siting of cooking equipment is recommended. Heavy equipment (such as deep freezers and refrigerators) should not be fixed in place in such a way that restricts access for cleaning. These items should be on lockable rollers and have flexible power, waste or water supply connections so that they can be moved to enable effective cleaning. Where equipment is not mobile it should be adequately sealed to the adjoining wall surface to eliminate dirt traps. Old equipment and items that are no longer in use, should be removed from the premises so as not to hamper cleaning of the surrounding area, or harbour dust/dirt.

Food Safety (General Food Hygiene) Regulations 1995 – Guide to compliance for Markets & Fairs

SCHEDULE 1
THE 'RULES OF HYGIENE'

Chapter VI   Food Waste

This section applies to ALL food businesses.

Legal requirement	Guide to compliance	Advice on good practice
1. Food waste and other refuse must not be allowed to accumulate in food rooms, except so far as is unavoidable for the proper functioning of the business.	Refuse and waste must not be allowed to accumulate on the floor. Any waste awaiting disposal later, must be kept in suitable containers that are emptied regularly and not allowed to overflow. If disposal facilities are not available on site then the bin must be large enough to hold waste produced during the trading period.	
2. Food waste and other refuse must be deposited in closeable containers unless the proprietor of the food business can satisfy the food authority that other types of containers used are appropriate. These containers must be of an appropriate construction, kept in sound condition, and where necessary be easy to clean and disinfect.	The internal and external surfaces of non-disposable waste containers must be washable and in good repair. For businesses where the only waste produced is dry waste, such as packaging, the waste container may not need to be lidded. Cardboard boxes must only be used for dry waste, such as packaging, and must be removed from the food area and disposed of at the end of each day. Refuse/waste must not be stored in any way that it will be an attraction to pests. Where liquid waste cannot be linked directly to the mains drainage system, holding tanks may be used (see below).	Plastic linings make removing rubbish and cleaning the bins easier. When rubbish is removed to a central storage area the plastic sack should be placed in a lidded, rodent and bird proof container. Where open food (other than whole fruit and vegetables) is handled, all bins should have foot, knee or elbow operated lids. Hand operated lids should not be used as these may be a source of contamination.
3. Adequate provision must be made for the removal and storage of food waste and other refuse. Refuse stores must be designed and managed in such a way as to enable them to be kept clean, and to protect against access by pests, and against contamination of food, drinking water, equipment or premises.	Central refuse stores provided by operators of markets or fairs must be: ● kept clean and tidy with daily washing of the opening to chutes and floor areas around chutes, skips, bins, and other soiled surfaces and equipment; ● managed and supervised in such a way that ensures it is kept clean and not misused; ● kept free from pests such as rats, mice, birds, flies and insects. Bins must be lidded, compactor areas must be physically separate from where food is stored, prepared or sold. Any accommodation must be proofed against access by pests. Regular cleaning must be carried out to reduce pest problems;	

- the area around refuse stores must be capable of being swilled down, kept clear of weeds and well lit;
- external refuse stores must be on a hardstanding to enable the area to be kept clean;
- liquid waste contained in holding tanks must be discharged carefully so that there is no risk of food contamination;
- run in compliance with the Water Industry Act 1991 section 111. This requires that nothing should be disposed of down drains connecting with a public sewer, which may damage the sewer, interfere with its free flow or the treatment and disposal of the sewage. In particular grease and oil must not be disposed of down drains but should be dealt with by a specialist contractor.

Sole traders in out of town locations must make their own adequate arrangements for waste storage and its removal from site after trading, to a suitable disposal point.

Sole traders who operate from a commercial or domestic base may make adequate refuse and collection arrangements at their base premises, such as a waste collection contract, and then return all their waste to that base.

Part 3   SCHEDULE 1
                THE 'RULES OF HYGIENE'

Chapter VII   Water Supply

This section applies to ALL food businesses.

Legal requirement	Guide to compliance	Advice on good practice
1. There must be an adequate supply of potable water.	Food businesses must ensure that they have an adequate supply of "potable" water (i.e. water that is safe to drink), as specified in Council Directive 80/778/EEC of 15th July, 1980 relating to the quality of water intended for human consumption.	
	Where available, food businesses will be able to use water that comes directly from a mains supply.	Water that comes from the mains supply can generally be assumed to be potable.
	If a mains supply is not available then food businesses may use containers of water which can be filled from the mains supply, water tanks/bowsers, or a private water supply. The food business operator must ensure this water is potable.	Where water is obtained from water tanks/bowsers or a private water supply the food business operator should obtain advice on the potability of the water from the market or fair operator, the land owner, or local food authority.
	Where the market or fair operator provides water tanks/bowsers they must ensure that they are regularly cleaned and disinfected and filled from a potable supply.	
	Where containers of water are used they must be:	Water containers should not be used for any other purpose. It is important to distinguish between "clean" water containers and "waste" water containers.
	● made of food grade materials and be enclosed;	
	● kept clean and disinfected frequently to avoid the risk of contamination;	
	● emptied and refilled regularly so as to avoid unacceptable contamination by micro-organisms;	It is good practice to empty water containers and refill with fresh potable water on a daily basis. They should be kept clean and be disinfected at least weekly together with any filling hoses that are used.
	● of sufficient capacity to store enough water for the businesses' potable water needs (unless they can be refilled from a potable supply on site).	Water containers should hold a minimum of 9 litres per person, working within the food business. This should be adequate for hand, equipment and food washing and other potable water uses.

Legal requirement	Guide to compliance	Advice on good practice

This potable water must be used whenever necessary to ensure foodstuffs are not contaminated.

Potable water must be used:

● for cleaning food;
● for cleaning surfaces which may come into contact with food;
● for cleaning hands;
● for including in food and drinks;
● for cooking of food;
● any other operations where there is a risk of contaminating foodstuffs.

2. Where appropriate, ice must be made from potable water. This ice must be used whenever necessary to ensure foodstuffs are not contaminated. It must be made, handled and stored under conditions which protect it from all contamination.

Any ice that will come into contact with food and drink must be made from potable water which meets the specifications referred to in Directive 80/778/EEC.

Ice machines must be regularly cleaned as must containers and utensils used to store and dispense ice. Parts of the ice machine and utensils which come into contact with ice must be disinfected at intervals.

Utensils must be made from durable materials that will not present a foreign body hazard from brittle fracture.

Ice buckets should have lids. Utensils (e.g. tongs) should be used to handle ice that will come into direct contact with food and drink.

3. Steam used directly in contact with food must not contain any substance which presents a hazard to health, or is likely to contaminate the product.

If steam, (e.g. from cleaning equipment) could contact food then the steam must be made from potable water.

4. Water unfit for drinking used for the generation of steam, refrigeration, fire control and other similar purposes not relating to food, must be conducted in separate systems, readily identifiable and having no connection with, nor any possibility of reflux into, the potable water systems.

Some premises may have non-potable water supplies (e.g. to supply hoses for fire fighting). These non-potable supplies must be clearly marked to indicate their use (e.g. for fire fighting only) and must not be used for cleaning.

It is recommended that the supply of non-potable water to food stalls is avoided.

Non-potable water supplies may be used for non-food applications (e.g. cleaning the exterior of vehicles).

Part 3   **SCHEDULE 1**
THE 'RULES OF HYGIENE'

Chapter VIII   Personal Hygiene

This section applies to ALL food businesses.

The requirements are a result of the recognition of the role that people may play in contaminating food. They place responsibilities on everyone working in a food handling area and on food business proprietors, and outline the action that they should take to prevent the contamination of food.

Staff who display poor personal hygiene not only pose a risk of causing food poisoning by contaminating food but will also offend customers leading to loss of business.

The legal requirements are contained in Schedule 1, Chapter VIII and regulation 5 of the Regulations.

Legal requirement	Guide to compliance	Advice on good practice
1. *Every person working in a food handling area shall maintain a high degree of personal cleanliness...*	This applies to 'every person' working in a food handling area whether or not they handle food. The proprietor must ensure that all staff observe good personal hygiene, and refrain from unhygienic habits and practices which may expose food to the risk of contamination. The following would fulfil the requirement: ● Washing hands regularly, particularly after going to the toilet, after handling raw food, after handling rubbish, before starting work, on returning to work, after sneezing/coughing. ● Not smoking, eating, drinking or chewing gum where open food is handled. ● Covering any spots, skin cuts and abrasions (on exposed areas such as hands or lower arms) with water proof dressings. ● Not wearing jewellery, nail varnish or false nails which may present a risk of contamination. As well as physically contaminating food itself, jewellery can harbour dirt and bacteria.	It is good practice to have a company 'code' of good hygiene practice available for staff and visitors (such as maintenance and enforcement officers) to follow. Notices emphasising the key points can be displayed in prominent positions. Signs should be displayed in or near toilets to remind users to wash their hands. Gloves should not be used as an alternative to hand washing. Smoking, eating or drinking should not be allowed in any food environment including warehouses or loading areas. Distinctively coloured waterproof dressings are easily seen if they fall off. Watches or chains should not be worn. Plain wedding bands and sleepers in pierced ears are acceptable.

Legal requirement	Guide to compliance	Advice on good practice

... and shall wear suitable, clean and, where appropriate, protective clothing.

The standard and type of protective clothing required will depend on the type of food handled and the duties carried out. The following would fulfil the requirement:

- Staff handling open food - suitable, clean, protective clothing (e.g. coat, jacket, uniform) and head covering containing the hair.
- Staff handling wrapped, canned, bottled goods or whole fruit and vegetables - suitable, clean clothing.

Protective clothing must be kept in good condition and changed when dirty, particularly when moving from a 'dirty' operation such as cleaning raw vegetables to a 'clean' operation such as making sandwiches.

Protective clothing should preferably cover the arms and body.

A suitable apron or coat over normal clothing is advisable.

It is good practice for all visitors to food handling areas to wear appropriate protective clothing and head covering.

Hair should be kept clean and tied back where possible.

Press studs are preferable to buttons which can easily fall off. All loose threads and buttons should be secured.

Spare sets of protective clothing should be available for when others are being washed.

Staff who handle/prepare open high risk food should not travel to work in their protective clothing. They should remove their protective clothing if they leave the premises, (e.g. during breaks, using the toilet or to smoke).

2. No person, known or suspected to be suffering from, or to be a carrier of, a disease likely to be transmitted through food or while affected, for example with infected wounds, skin infections, sores or with diarrhoea, shall be permitted to work in any food handling area in any capacity in which there is any likelihood of directly or indirectly contaminating food with pathogenic micro-organisms.

The food business proprietor has a duty to take appropriate action as soon as he/she suspects or becomes aware that a member of staff is suffering from any of the conditions listed. This may involve temporary exclusion from work or exclusion from specific duties. Alternative duties must not involve any likelihood of directly or indirectly contaminating food e.g. direct contact with open food, surfaces and equipment in areas where open food is stored or processed, or high risk food handlers.

Staff should only return to work when they can show that the illness no longer presents a risk.

A proprietor should also ensure that all staff are aware of which illnesses should be reported, how to report them and who to report to.

Staff returning to work after illness should be reminded that **good personal hygiene must be observed on their return to work**. If there is any doubt about excluding someone from work or a person's suitability for return to work, advice should be sought from a doctor or the local Environmental Health Department.

Separately, under regulation 5, any person working in a food handling area must report certain illnesses or conditions to the proprietor where there is any likelihood of them directly or indirectly contaminating food. They must immediately report if they:

- know or suspect that they are suffering from or are a carrier of a disease likely to be transmitted through food; or
- are afflicted with an infected wound, skin infection, sores, diarrhoea, or any analogous medical condition such as stomach upset or vomiting.

Staff concerned should inform their manager, supervisor or the proprietor before starting work.

A medical questionnaire may be used prior to appointing new staff to assess whether or not they are fit to work with food. An example of a questionnaire is contained in Appendix D.

Further guidance on staff health is contained in 'Food Handlers: Fitness to Work' from the Department of Health. See References, page 145.

SCHEDULE 1
THE 'RULES OF HYGIENE'

Chapter IX   **Provisions Applicable To Foodstuffs**

This section applies to ALL food businesses.

Legal requirement	Guide to compliance	Advice on good practice
1. No raw materials or ingredients shall be accepted by a food business if they are known to be, or might reasonably be expected to be, so contaminated with parasites, pathogenic micro-organisms, or toxic, decomposed or foreign substances, that after normal sorting and/or preparatory or processing procedures hygienically applied by food businesses, they would still be unfit for human consumption.	Routine checks must be made periodically on deliveries of food. Check 'use by' dates of foods that have them. Do not accept foods past their 'use by' date. If you suspect that a batch of food is substandard and that even after sorting the majority will be unfit, you must not bring it or accept it on the stall, vehicle or handcart. Any unfit food discovered after unpacking must be labelled as unfit and set to one side (if it is to be used as evidence of a claim or further action). The food must be kept in such a manner so as not to expose any other foods to a risk of contamination. The food must not be sold for human consumption and staff must be made aware of this. The food must be removed from the stall as soon as possible and destroyed unless it is to be used as evidence. Food would be "unfit for human consumption" if it was putrid or toxic or if, for example it contained very unpleasant foreign material. Meat would be unfit if it was taken from animals slaughtered in a knackers yard. Food would be "injurious to health" if it was contaminated with toxic materials or pathogenic micro-organisms at levels which may cause harm in a substantial part of the population. It could be "unfit" even if the harm were cumulative or only became apparent over a long period of time. An ingredient which showed up as an intolerant reaction in only a few individuals would not be covered.	Check that frozen or chilled foods are delivered at the right temperatures. See Part 4 Temperature Control page 52. If possible check your suppliers' premises and specify your food and delivery requirements. Perishable foods should be accepted onto the stall with enough 'shelf life' to enable you to sell them. It is not good practice to use/sell food past its 'best before' date. The local authority Environmental Health Department may be contacted to investigate any contravention of food safety legislation by suppliers, or to accept the voluntary surrender of unfit food. A charge may be made but the cost of wasted food may be covered by your insurance. There are some foods to which a small number of sensitive individuals have an intolerant reaction or allergy. If an ingredient used is known to cause an intolerant reaction (e.g. nuts) you should consider indicating that it is present in the product.

Legal requirement	Guide to compliance	Advice on good practice
	Food would be "contaminated in such a way that it would be unreasonable to expect it to be consumed in that state" if it contained, for example, substantial residues of antibiotics, or unpleasant foreign material, or significant solvent residues.	
2. Raw materials and ingredients stored in the establishment shall be kept in appropriate conditions designed to prevent harmful deterioration and to protect them from contamination.	If you store food on your stall or vehicle or have a warehouse, you must ensure that the food cannot become contaminated and is stored in conditions to prevent harmful deterioration. Storage areas must be clean and tidy and kept free from pests. Raw foods must be stored with adequate separation from ready to eat foods to prevent cross contamination. Temperature control of the food may be required. See Part 4, Temperature Control, page 52.	Part-used packs should be put in suitable lidded containers. Once canned food has been opened you should not use the can for storage. Food not for immediate use should be decanted into suitable plastic or ceramic containers. These foods may now require refrigeration and should be used within the time period required or recommended. It is good practice to label the container with a date by which the food should be used. Good stock rotation is essential for foods with 'use by' dates and is important in ensuring the quality of other foods. Spillages in storage areas should be cleared away as soon as possible so as not to attract pests. Operate a 'clean as you go' policy.
3. All food which is handled, stored, packaged, displayed and transported, shall be protected against any contamination likely to render the food unfit for human consumption, injurious to health or contaminated in such a way that it would be unreasonable to expect it to be consumed in that state. In particular, food must be so placed and/or protected as to minimize any risk of contamination.	All food that you are responsible for must be protected to ensure it is fit and safe to eat and that all food you sell is in a condition that you can reasonably expect someone to eat. See guidance on terms 'unfit', 'injurious to health' and 'contaminated' on page 42. For example: ● it is not acceptable to have fruit or vegetables that are a mixture of partly rotted and sound food and to sell that mixture to the consumer; ● it is not acceptable to sell open ready to eat food that is visibly contaminated with dust, dirt or mould.	

Legal requirement	Guide to compliance	Advice on good practice

High risk foods must be stored and displayed so that they cannot be contaminated by raw foods or by external sources.

This may involve all or any of the following:

- physical separation of raw and ready to eat foods;
- protection from public coughing or sneezing over food by providing a "sneeze screen";
- designing/siting displays or display equipment to avoid customers/staff reaching over food;
- not allowing animals on the food premises/stall/vehicle;
- placing food off the ground;
- good staff personal hygiene. See Part 3, Chapter IX, Personal Hygiene, page 39.

A minimum height of 45 cm above the ground is recommended.

Methods of handling food must also protect it against harmful contamination, with particular emphasis on micro-organisms with a low infective dose.

The guidance concerning cross contamination may be updated in the light of specific Government legislative proposals implementing the Pennington Group recommendations for the control of E.coli 0157.

Adequate procedures must be in place to ensure pests are controlled.

You must not allow food to be contaminated by pests including insects, rats, mice and birds. You must have a procedure to control any pests that could gain access. This procedure could be:

either -

A contract with a pest control operator to regularly survey the premises and carry out any necessary treatment and proofing work.

or -

You carrying out regular checks of food and premises for the presence of pests and taking the necessary steps to deal with any problems.

It is advisable to keep written records of pest control surveys, treatments and proofing work. This may help to show that "due diligence" has been taken to prevent an infestation of pests.

Where it is impracticable to screen openings in enclosed premises, against flying insects, it may be appropriate to use an electric flying insect killer. This should not be sited over open food and should be emptied and maintained according to the manufacturer's instructions. These devices should not be used as an alternative to screening against flying insects.

Legal requirement	Guide to compliance	Advice on good practice
4. *Hazardous and/or inedible substances, including animal feedstuffs, shall be adequately labelled and stored in separate and secure containers.*	Unfit food and waste food must be disposed of as soon as possible. If it is necessary to keep some of this food on the premises, stall, vehicle or handcart, it must be clearly labelled, (e.g. 'not for human consumption').	
	Open pet food must be kept separate from open food intended for human consumption.	
	Cleaning materials and chemicals must be labelled and kept away from food.	Chemicals should be used, stored and handled safely in accordance with the Control of Substances Hazardous to Health Regulations 1994.
	Cleaning materials or other hazardous chemicals must **never** be put into empty drinks bottles or food containers.	
	Poisons used for pest control purposes must be in clearly labelled containers and located so that they cannot contaminate food. Chemicals used to spray premises must either be suitable for use in a food room or the treated area must not be used as a food room until it is safe to do so.	Advice should be sought from a pest control contractor about the suitability of chemicals used.

Part 3 **SCHEDULE 1**
THE 'RULES OF HYGIENE'

Chapter X **Food Hygiene Supervision, Instruction And/Or Training**

This section applies to ALL food businesses.

Legal Requirement

Schedule 1 Chapter X and regulation 4 (2) (d):
"The proprietor of a food business shall ensure that food handlers engaged in the food business are supervised and instructed and/or trained in food hygiene matters commensurate with their work activities".

Objective of the Regulation

This is a new legal requirement. It takes a flexible approach to food hygiene supervision, instruction and training and allows the proprietors of food businesses to fulfil their duty by assessing the needs of themselves and their staff, based on, for example:

i) the nature of food handled by each person,
ii) the food handling operations undertaken,
iii) the level of supervision available and the level of responsibility staff and proprietors have.

NOTE   The legal requirement applies only to a "food handler" which means:
"Any person involved in a food business who handles food in the course of their work, or as part of their duties, to any extent, whether the food is open or pre-wrapped". [Food includes drink and ice]

Legal requirement	Guide to compliance	Advice on good practice
The proprietor of a food business shall ensure that food handlers engaged in the food business are supervised and instructed and/or trained in food hygiene matters commensurate with their work activities.	**Supervision** **All** food handlers must be appropriately supervised to ensure that they work hygienically. Close supervision will be necessary for new, casual and temporary staff until they are fully trained. Staff handling high risk foods will need to be more closely supervised than those handling low risk foods. Staff who have been trained and/or instructed or claim to have been trained must be supervised to ensure that the training or instruction is being put into practice.	Supervision should be used to assess when any refresher training or instruction is necessary, by identifying bad hygiene practices and lack of understanding of food hygiene principles.

Legal requirement	Guide to compliance	Advice on good practice

Instruction

All food handlers must receive instruction to ensure that they work hygienically.

In particular they must receive written or verbal induction instruction before commencing any food handling activities. The induction instructions must include:

● the standards of personal hygiene expected;
● the need to inform management of any illness or circumstances that could pose a risk to the hygienic operation of the business.

This will include the relevant details in Personal Hygiene, see pages 39-41.

All employees must receive hygiene instructions specific to their activities. The instructions must cover food hazards and those control measures identified by the hazard analysis of their work activities. This must be given before the particular work activities are carried out and revised as a result of any change in job practices.
For further details see Table I - Examples of Specific Food Handling Activities Which Require Hygiene Instructions, page 48.

Training

The need for structured training depends on the risk to food safety, and training must be provided for different staff in accordance with Table II, page 49. The training required takes into account the problem of high staff turnover.

The training does not have to be delivered by an accredited training body but must be of an appropriate standard. It may be organised in-house, through distance learning, or through outside training organisations (e.g. certified food hygiene courses, NVQs or other formal courses to the required level).

Specific instruction or training must be given to staff handling pre-wrapped high risk food on the need for temperature control and stock rotation.

Advice on good practice column:

Instruction should, where possible, include an explanation of why the measures are necessary and how they ensure food safety. This may encourage compliance through understanding the need to protect food from harmful contamination, to protect consumers and prevent the spread of disease. This is particularly important for casual or temporary staff who are not 'trained'.

It is good practice to provide both induction and job specific instruction to non-food handlers, who work in food premises on cleaning or other support activities. Instruction would concentrate on the way their activities may impinge on food safety (e.g. personal hygiene).

Instructions should be repeated at suitable intervals or explained as necessary, as indicated by the observations of supervision.

Training is aimed at ensuring that individual staff understand why certain precautions are necessary. It is good practice, therefore, to train all food handlers in food hygiene principles relevant to their job, in order to reduce the amount of supervision necessary.

Supervisors, managers or proprietors who are not food handlers, but may have a direct influence on the hygienic operation of the business, should receive structured training to levels 1, 2 or 3 as appropriate. See Table III, page 50 for details of these levels.

Table I outlines examples of hygiene instructions that may be necessary for staff, depending on their food handling activities. There may be additional instructions identified by hazard analysis.

TABLE I
Examples of Specific Food Handling Activities Which Require Hygiene Instructions

1	Stock rotation and date labelling procedures.
2	Procedures to prevent cross contamination when handling and storing raw and cooked foods.
3	Responsibilities and procedures for cleaning and/or disinfection.
4	Requirements for hygienic and efficient use of refrigerated storage/display units.
5	Procedures for dealing with unfit and out of date foods and in catering operations, surplus or previously prepared food.
6	Responsibilities and procedures for reporting defects regarding the structure of the premises or equipment or signs of pest infestation.
7	Responsibilities for monitoring critical control points (e.g. monitoring the temperature of hot holding/refrigeration equipment).
8	Any supervisory responsibilities.
9	Awareness of any other hazards and control measures identified by a hazard analysis.
	ALL STAFF MUST KNOW HOW TO DO THEIR JOB HYGIENICALLY

Table II outlines the structured training that should be undertaken by different categories of staff, based on the type of food handled, their supervisory responsibilities and whether they are casual and/or temporary staff.

TABLE II Requirement For Structured Training		
Category of Staff	**Guide to Compliance**	**Advice on Good Practice**
A Staff who <u>only</u> handle low risk open foods or pre-wrapped, canned or bottled goods.	Supervision and instruction must be undertaken as in Table I.	Training in any specific risks and precautions required in their job will encourage good practice.
B Staff who handle open high risk food.	Structured training equivalent to level 1 must be undertaken. See Table III, page 50 for details.	Refresher training may be necessary at intervals, its frequency based on the competence and experience of the individual and their level of involvement in controlling critical points.
C Food handlers who also have a supervisory role (irrespective of type of food handled).	Structured training equivalent to level 1 must be undertaken. See Table III, page 50.	Structured training to levels 2 and/or 3 depending on responsibility. See Table III, page 50.
D Food handlers employed as casual or temporary staff.	The training requirements will depend on whether they are category A, B or C staff. The training requirements specified for these categories must be complied with, unless close supervision and good instruction of these staff are practical, are carried out and can ensure good hygiene practices.	Employ staff with previous food hygiene training if possible. Supervision will still be necessary to ensure training is being put into practice. Where high staff turnover makes the cost of structured training prohibitive then casual or temporary staff should be deployed on low-risk tasks unless they have been trained.

Table III indicates appropriate contents of structured training to levels 1, 2 and 3 referred to previously. Level I is suitable for all food handling staff. Level 2 is suitable for supervisors, managers and proprietors of small and medium scale food businesses. Level 3 is suitable for managers and proprietors of large scale food businesses.

TABLE III		
Core Food Hygiene Training Elements		
LEVEL 1	LEVEL 2	LEVEL 3
Causes of food poisoning, its symptoms and prevention. Sources of food contamination and its prevention. Personal hygiene. Elementary design and construction of food premises. Cleaning and disinfection. Pest identification and control. Food storage and temperature control. Food processing and temperature control.	As Level 1. *Plus the following elements of supervisory management:* Their role in maintaining communications and monitoring workplace standards. Importance of, and application of hazard identification and control and monitoring processes and procedures. Monitoring staff hygiene practices.	As Levels 1 and 2. *Plus the following elements of management:* Knowledge of legislation relating to their business. Knowledge and ability to establish and control food hygiene management systems for example: i) Personal hygiene and staff training; ii) cleaning and disinfection; iii) pest control; iv) food purchasing and acceptance procedures; v) equipment and premises selection, design, maintenance and alteration; vi) food storage procedures.

Further Advice on Good Practice

It is a useful aid to the management of food hygiene supervision, instruction and training to have a training/instruction plan and to keep records of any training or instruction undertaken, or supervisory measures for each member of staff. These plans and records may also contribute to any 'due diligence' defence under the Food Safety Act 1990. The training plan should include an assessment of staff skills and knowledge; the skills and knowledge necessary for their work activities and therefore the supervision, instruction and training necessary for each member of staff. Where appropriate, a timetable should be drawn up for new and existing staff. The need for refresher training and training arising from changes of duty, responsibility, foods handled or handling procedures or controls should be included. Training on-site can be very effective, provided it is free from distractions and the normal pressures of work, as the material being taught can be related directly to the work situation.

Where businesses decide in-house training is beyond their resources or capabilities, a range of accredited food hygiene courses are available. Organisations offering these courses include:

- The Chartered Institute of Environmental Health (CIEH)
- The Royal Environmental Health Institute of Scotland (REHIS)
- The Royal Institute of Public Health and Hygiene (RIPHH)
- The Royal Society of Health (RSH)
- The Society of Food Hygiene Technology (SOFHT)
- The Mobile and Outside Caterers Association (MOCA)

For further information on courses available contact the organisations concerned (see pages 142 - 144 for addresses).

Special arrangements may be necessary for persons whose first language is not English or those with literacy or learning difficulties. This may involve the use of translators, experienced trainers and extending the training period.

Part 4   THE FOOD SAFETY (TEMPERATURE CONTROL) REGULATIONS 1995

Introduction

These Regulations recognise the importance of correct temperature control in restricting the growth of bacteria and minimising the risk of food poisoning. Generally, bacteria will not grow, or will grow very slowly, at temperatures below 8°C and are generally killed by temperatures above 63°C. Temperature conditions of between 8°C and 63°C will usually allow bacteria to grow and should, therefore, be avoided.

The main aim of the Temperature Regulations is to ensure certain foods which are likely to support the growth of harmful bacteria (pathogenic), which may cause food poisoning, are kept at the correct temperature. Foods which are likely to be subject to temperature control are referred to as 'relevant' foods and are listed in Table IV, page 64, at the end of this chapter.

The Temperature Regulations apply to these foods at all stages of transport, preparation, processing, storage and display for sale during manufacture, retail and catering.

It must be noted that the temperatures referred to in the Temperature Regulations refer to the temperature of the food, not the air temperature of its container.

The need for temperature control should be considered as part of the hazard analysis requirements of regulation 4(3) of the Food Safety (General Food Hygiene) Regulations 1995. Also, an understanding of the importance of chill control should be an element in the training of staff involved in food handling.

The Temperature Regulations provide exemptions from the chill and hot holding requirements in certain circumstances. It is the responsibility of the food business to satisfy themselves that a food will qualify for one of the exemptions. If storage information is not available on the label and there is any doubt as to the correct storage requirements for a particular product, advice should be sought from the supplier and/or manufacturer.

The following guidance is applicable in England and Wales and is followed by specific requirements applicable to Scotland.

TEMPERATURE CONTROL REQUIREMENTS FOR ENGLAND AND WALES

Legal requirement	Guide to compliance	Advice on good practice

Chill holding requirements

4.-(1) Subject to paragraph (2) and Regulation 5, no person shall keep any food -

(a) which is likely to support the growth of pathogenic micro-organisms or the formation of toxins; and

This Regulation only applies to food that will support the growth of pathogenic micro-organisms or the formation of toxins. See Table IV, page 64.

(b) with respect to which any commercial operation is being carried out,

All these foods must be kept at or below 8°C, except where they are covered by one of the exemptions listed below.

at or in food premises at a temperature above 8°C.

It is the temperature of the food, which should be at or below 8°C, not the temperature of the refrigerator. It is good practice to operate refrigerators at 5°C to allow a margin of error below the legal standard.

Temperature monitoring and logging is an important means of ensuring compliance with the Temperature Regulations. Thermometers or equipment with a temperature display should be available for this. A probe thermometer is desirable to check internal food temperatures. This should be disinfected before and after use. Written records indicate good practice to food enforcement officers and help to identify any problems due to faulty equipment or bad practice. See Appendix B.

Foods which are not likely to support the growth of pathogenic micro-organisms or the formation of toxins are not covered by this requirement.

Checks should always be made with the food manufacturer if there is any doubt as to whether or not it can support the growth of harmful bacteria or the formation of toxins. Some foods(e.g. hard cheeses) may be chilled for quality reasons rather than food safety reasons. There is no requirement to have a refrigerator. If relevant food can be kept at or below 8°C by other means,(e.g. insulated boxes and frozen ice packs), then this will be acceptable.

(2) Paragraph (1) shall not apply to any food which, as part of a mail order transaction, is being conveyed by post or by a private or common carrier to an ultimate consumer.

The subject of mail order foods is beyond the scope of this Guide.

Market traders are unlikely to be 'ultimate consumers' so any mail order food must be delivered to market traders at the correct temperature.

Legal requirement	Guide to compliance	Advice on good practice
(3) Subject to regulation 5, no person shall supply by mail order any food which - (a) is likely to support the growth of pathogenic micro-organisms or the formation of toxins; and (b) is being or has been conveyed by post or by a private or common carrier to an ultimate consumer, at a temperature which has given rise to or is likely to give rise to a risk to health.	The subject of mail order foods is beyond the scope of this Guide.	When traders receive any food listed in Table IV, page 64, by mail order, they must be assured it is safe and has not been exposed to adverse temperature conditions. If there are no such assurances, the food should not be accepted.

Food Safety (Temperature Control) Regulations 1995 – Guide to compliance for Markets & Fairs

Legal requirement	Guide to compliance	Advice on good practice

General Exemptions from the Chill Holding Requirements.

5. *Regulation 4 shall not apply to -*

(a) food which -

(i) has been cooked or re-heated,
(ii) is for service or on display for sale, and
(iii) needs to be kept hot in order to control the growth of pathogenic micro-organisms or the formation of toxins;

These are the general exemptions from the chill holding requirements of 8°C for food which is intended to be sold hot. These are covered in regulation 8.

(b) food which, for the duration of its shelf life, may be kept at ambient temperatures with no risk to health;

Some perishable foods may be kept at ambient (room) temperature for the duration of their shelf life without posing a risk to health. This may be because they are packed in a certain way,(e.g. under vacuum for certain foods) or because they are only intended to have a short shelf life.

Always consult the label for advice on storage temperatures.

Certain bakery products may benefit from specific exemptions stemming from this provision. These are detailed in the Guide for the baking industry.

Cooked pies and pasties containing meat, fish (or any substitute for meat or fish), vegetables or cheese, (or any combination of these) encased in pastry to which nothing has been added after baking (e.g. gelatine) and sausage rolls, may be safely stored and displayed at ambient (room) temperature, on the day of their production or the next day (i.e. up to a maximum of 48 hours).

Uncut baked egg custards and curd tarts may be kept at ambient (room) temperature for up to 24 hours after production.

Once cut the products must be stored at 8°C or below (in England and Wales). After the expiry of the time exemptions, the products must be disposed of; they cannot be given an extended shelf life by then chilling them to 8°C or below.

Temperature control may be required on hot days if ambient temperatures are so high that foodstuffs would be kept at temperatures which would result in a risk to health.

It is important to obtain information from suppliers and/or manufacturers on when these products were produced. If in doubt, keep them chilled. It is good practice to keep these foods chilled where possible, as the quality will be maintained.

Legal requirement	Guide to compliance	Advice on good practice
(c) food which is being or has been subjected to a process such as dehydration or canning intended to prevent the growth of pathogenic micro-organisms at ambient temperatures, but this paragraph shall cease to apply in circumstances where - *(i) after or by virtue of that process the food was contained in a hermetically sealed container, and* *(ii) that container has been opened;*	This applies to relevant food which has been subjected to a process designed to prevent the growth of harmful bacteria (e.g. canning or dehydration). However, once a can has been opened or water added to a dehydrated product, the exemption ceases to apply (e.g. rehydrated pasta would be likely to support the growth of micro-organisms or toxin formation and therefore must be chilled). Some canned meats are only pasteurised rather than fully sterilised and must therefore be kept chilled, even in the unopened can.	Food from opened cans should be placed in clean, lidded containers during chilled storage. Labels will help indicate when the can was opened and the type of food. It is good practice to remove high acid canned foods, (e.g. tomatoes), from the can to avoid the acid attacking the metal and contaminating the food.
(d) food which must be ripened or matured at ambient temperatures, but this paragraph shall cease to apply once the process of ripening or maturation is completed;	This exemption applies to foods which can only be ripened or matured at ambient temperatures (e.g. soft, mould-ripened cheeses such as Brie, Camembert and Stilton), and only applies until the ripening process is complete.	The ripening or maturation of food is more likely to occur during the manufacturing process. These products are likely to require storage at or below 8°C at wholesalers and retailers.
(e) raw food intended for further processing (which includes cooking) before human consumption, but only if that processing, if undertaken correctly, will render that food fit for human consumption;	This exemption applies to <u>raw</u> food which will be thoroughly cooked or otherwise processed before consumption, (e.g. fresh meat and fish), but see (f) below. The exemption does not apply to fresh meat or fish which is intended to be eaten raw, (e.g. steak tartare or fish for sushi) - these will still need to be kept at or below 8°C. Raw scrombroid fish (e.g. tuna and mackerel) are not exempted by this section because the 'scrombrotoxin' is not destroyed by heat and cooking will not render contaminated food fit for human consumption.	It is good practice to keep raw meat and fish chilled, to reduce the growth of food spoilage organisms and pathogens and to preserve the quality of the food. The appearance of chilled meat and fish is usually more appealing to the customer.
(f) food to which Council Regulation (EEC) No. 1906/90 on certain marketing standards for poultry, as amended, applies;	This Regulation requires fresh poultry meat (chicken, ducks, geese, turkey and guinea fowl) to be kept and/or displayed for sale at a temperature not exceeding 4°C or less than -2°C. Frozen poultry meat should not exceed -12°C, or -18°C for quick-frozen poultry meat. These temperatures are applicable at retail and wholesale level.	
(g) food to which Council Regulation (EEC) No. 1907/90 on certain marketing standards for eggs, as amended, applies.	This Regulation does not impose any temperature control requirement for shell eggs at retail or wholesale level.	It is good practice to keep eggs chilled and use them by their 'best before' date.

Food Safety (Temperature Control) Regulations 1995 – Guide to compliance for Markets & Fairs

Legal requirement	Guide to compliance	Advice on good practice

Upward variation of the 8°C temperature by manufacturers etc.

6.-(1)

In any proceedings for an offence of contravening regulation 4(1), it shall be a defence for a person charged (for the purposes of this regulation called "the defendant") to prove that -

(a) a food business responsible for manufacturing, preparing or processing the food has recommended that it is kept-

(i) at or below a specified temperature between 8°C and ambient temperatures, and
(ii) for a period not exceeding a specified shelf life;

(b) that recommendation has, unless the defendant is that food business, been communicated to the defendant either by means of a label on the packaging of the food or by means of some other appropriate form of written instruction;

(c) the food was not kept by the defendant at a temperature above the specified temperature; and

(d) at the time of the commission of the alleged offence, the specified shelf life had not been exceeded.

(2) A food business responsible for manufacturing, preparing or processing food shall not recommend that any food is kept -

(a) at or below a specified temperature between 8°C and ambient temperatures; and
(b) for a period not exceeding a specified shelf life,

unless that recommendation is supported by a well-founded scientific assessment of the safety of the food at the specified temperature.

This Regulation allows food businesses which are responsible for manufacturing, preparing or processing relevant food (e.g. caterer, baker) to recommend that any food is kept at or below a specified temperature between 8°C and ambient temperatures, for a set period of time, not exceeding its shelf life. They can only do this if they can provide a well-founded scientific assessment of the safety of the food under these circumstances. Details must then be passed onto food businesses by means of labelling or some other appropriate form of written instruction. Food businesses can then store these products under the conditions specified, for the duration of their shelf life.

If intending to use this defence a well-founded scientific assessment should be obtained from a food laboratory or consultant.

Food businesses can still choose to keep these foods at or below 8°C.

More detailed advice on scientific assessments is given in the 'Guidance on the Food Safety (Temperature Control) Regulations 1995', produced by the Department of Health. See References, page 146.

Legal requirement	Guide to compliance	Advice on good practice

Chill holding tolerance periods

7.-(1) In any proceedings for an offence of contravening regulation 4(1), it shall be a defence for a person charged to prove that the food -
(a) was for service or on display for sale;
(b) had not previously been kept for service or on display for sale at a temperature above 8°C or, in appropriate circumstances, the recommended temperature; and
(c) had been kept for service or on display for sale for a period of less than four hours.

(2) In any proceedings for an offence of contravening regulation 4(1), it shall be a defence for the person charged to prove that the food -

(a) was being transferred -
(i) to a vehicle used for the purposes of the activities of a food business from, or
(ii) from a vehicle used for the purposes of the activities of a food business to, premises (which includes vehicles) at which the food was going to be kept at or below 8°C or, in appropriate circumstances, the recommended temperature; or
(b) was kept at a temperature above 8°C or, in appropriate circumstances, the recommended temperature for an unavoidable reason, such as -
(i) to accommodate the practicalities of handling during and after processing or preparation,
(ii) the defrosting of equipment, or
(iii) temporary breakdown of equipment,
and was kept at a temperature above 8°C or, in appropriate circumstances, the recommended temperature for a limited period only and that period was consistent with food safety.

This Regulation provides an exemption from the requirement to keep relevant foods at or below 8°C, where that food is displayed for a **single period** of up to 4 hours to allow for service or display. At the end of this 4 hour period, the food must be cooled as quickly as possible and stored at or below 8°C or discarded. It must not be kept above 8°C again as the exemption is only for a 'single period', thus relevant foods must not have been stored/displayed at or above 8°C previously.

This Regulation makes allowances for the temperature of relevant food to rise above 8°C due to certain, unavoidable, reasons. These include - transfer to or from a vehicle; efficient handling during or after processing; defrosting of equipment or temporary breakdown of equipment. The time the food is above 8°C must be consistent with food safety. The length of the 'limited period' and permitted temperature rises are not specified by the Regulations but under normal circumstances a single limited period of up to 2 hours outside of temperature control is unlikely to be questioned.

It is essential to have good management of food displays to avoid exceeding the 4 hour exemption period:
● the amount of food on display should be kept to a minimum;
● good stock rotation is essential when re-stocking displays to ensure 'older' food is moved to the top of the pile;
● labelling and/or documentation will indicate when food went on display;
● constant checking of labels is essential to ensure the 4 hour period is not exceeded.

Avoid topping up 'bulk' displays as food on the bottom may be left for longer than 4 hours.

Every effort should be made to keep the time relevant food is outside of temperature control as short as possible.

When shopping for relevant foods, it is good practice to use cool bags/boxes with ice blocks and to put the food into chilled storage as soon as possible.

The breakdown of equipment can be avoided by routine maintenance checks.

Food Safety (Temperature Control) Regulations 1995 – Guide to compliance for Markets & Fairs

Legal requirement	Guide to compliance	Advice on good practice

Hot holding requirements

8. No person shall in the course of the activities of a food business keep any food which -

(a) has been cooked or reheated;

(b) is for service or on display for sale; and

(c) needs to be kept hot in order to control the growth of pathogenic micro-organisms or the formation of toxins,

at or in food premises at a temperature below 63°C.

This Regulation applies to foods similar in nature to the 'relevant' foods listed in Table IV, page 64 and requires that they must be kept hot, at 63°C or above.

Temperature monitoring equipment (e.g. probe thermometers), should be available to check that food is being kept at or above 63°C. It is good practice to check the food temperatures throughout the day and to write them down.

Probe thermometers should be disinfected before and after use.

Hot food display cabinets are not designed to heat food from cold. They are generally designed to hold hot food at 63°C or above. Relevant food should therefore be heated to 63°C or above before being placed in these cabinets.

Hot holding defences

9.-(1) In any proceedings for an offence of contravening regulation 8, it shall be a defence for a person charged to prove that -
(a) a well-founded scientific assessment of the safety of the food at temperatures below 63°C has concluded that there is no risk to health if, after cooking or reheating, the food is held for service or on display for sale -

(i) at a holding temperature which is below 63°C, and
(ii) for a period not exceeding a specified period of time; and

(b) at the time of the commission of the alleged offence, the food was held in a manner which is justified in the light of that scientific assessment.

The requirement in regulation 8, above, to keep relevant food at or above 63°C can be varied provided it is based on a well-founded scientific assessment. This is similar to the provisions in regulation 6 for chilled foods.

Anyone wishing to use this defence should seek expert advice. Although there is no requirement for this to be in the form of written instructions, it is advisable to get details of any scientific assessment in writing.

(2) In any proceedings for an offence of contravening regulation 8, it shall be a defence for a person charged to prove that the food -

(a) had been kept for service or on display for sale for a period of less than two hours; and

(b) had not previously been kept for service or on display for sale by that person.

This allows relevant food to be kept for service or on display at temperatures below 63°C for a **single period** of up to 2 hours. At the end of this 2 hour period, food must be restored to a suitable temperature (at or above 63°C or at or below 8°C) or discarded. It must not be kept on display, or kept for service, at a temperature below 63°C again. The exemption is for a 'single period' so relevant foods must not have been stored/displayed below 63°C previously.

Good management of food displays is essential. The burden of proof lies with the food business to show that the time limit has not been exceeded and that the food has not previously been used for service or display at or below 63°C. It is therefore advisable to monitor the temperature of the food and keep records of the times it went on display or for service.

Avoid topping up 'bulk displays' as food on the bottom may be left for longer than 2 hours.

Legal requirement	Guide to compliance	Advice on good practice

General requirement for food which is a risk to health

10.-(1) Subject to paragraph (2), no person shall in the course of the activities of a food business keep foodstuffs which are - **(a) raw materials, ingredients, intermediate products or finished products; and** **(b) likely to support the growth of pathogenic micro-organisms or the formation of toxins,** **at temperatures which would result in a risk to health.**	This is an overriding general requirement to keep relevant food at 'safe temperatures' and it applies to all forms of temperature control, including chill control and hot holding. In most circumstances, food businesses complying with the more specific requirement to keep food at or below 8°C or at 63°C or above will also be complying with this Regulation.	It is advisable to follow the storage and preparation advice given on the product label.
(2) Consistent with food safety, limited periods outside temperature control are permitted where necessary to accommodate the practicalities of handling during preparation, transport, storage, display and service of food.	This allows for limited periods outside temperature control, where necessary, for handling during preparation, transport, storage, display and service of relevant foods. Under no circumstances must these periods be so long that they compromise the safety of the food.	Relevant food should be temperature controlled until it is ready for use, (e.g. baked potato fillings, sandwich ingredients should be kept under refrigeration and only small quantities removed each time).
(3) A person may contravene paragraph (1) notwithstanding that he complies with the requirements of regulations 4 and 8, and in particular the keeping of perishable foodstuffs at above a maximum storage temperature recommended in any special storage conditions for them may be in contravention of paragraph (1) notwithstanding that they are kept at a temperature of 8°C or below.	There may be instances where a maximum temperature of less than 8°C is applicable and this will be indicated on the product label. Where this lower temperature is necessary for food safety reasons, that food must be kept at that temperature. When a lower temperature is specified only to preserve the quality of the food, the recommended temperature will not be a legal requirement.	Always consult the supplier/manufacturer for advice on storage conditions if there is any doubt. Advice on product labels should always be followed.

Legal requirement	Guide to compliance	Advice on good practice

Cooling of Food

11. *A food business responsible for cooling any food which must, by virtue of this Part, be kept at a temperature below ambient temperatures shall cool that food as quickly as possible following -*

(a) the final heat processing stage; or

(b) if no heat process is applied, the final preparation stage,

to the temperature at which, by virtue of this Part, it must be kept.

This Regulation requires that the temperature of all relevant food be reduced to 8°C or below (or to a higher temperature as provided for in regulation 6), as quickly as possible after cooking or after its final preparation stage.

When food has become hot during processing/preparation, it is better to allow it to cool to ambient temperatures before being placed into a refrigerator.

Food which is cooling to ambient temperatures must not be placed so it is at risk of contamination.

Food which has reached ambient temperature during preparation must be returned to the refrigerator as quickly as possible.

It is good practice to allow hot food to cool for no longer than 4 hours before refrigerating it. Large quantities of food will cool quicker if they are split into smaller portions and placed in a cool, well ventilated place. Ice made from potable water can be added to dishes to aid cooling. Placing food in cold containers on cold surfaces (e.g. stone, tiles, metal) will aid rapid cooling.

Legal requirement	Guide to compliance	Advice on good practice

Guides to good hygiene practice

12. For the purposes of regulations 6 (2) and 9 (1), the presence of a scientific assessment of the safety of any food in a guide to good hygiene practice which has been -

(a) forwarded by the Secretary of State to the Commission pursuant to article 5.5 of the Directive, unless the Secretary of State has announced that the guide no longer complies with article 3 of the Directive; or

(b) developed in accordance with article 5.6 and 7 of the Directive and published in accordance with article 5.8 of the Directive,

shall, until the contrary is proved, be considered sufficient evidence that the scientific assessment in question is well-founded.

This Regulation states that if there is any scientific assessment, which allows relevant foods to be kept above 8°C or below 63°C, and which appears in an Industry Guide to Good Hygiene Practice, then that scientific assessment will be considered as 'well-founded'.

There are no such assessments in this Guide.

TABLE IV

Types of Foods Which Require Chilled Storage

The following list provides **examples** of various foods which, under normal conditions of storage and use, and in the absence of adequate preserving factors, should be kept chilled to help secure food safety. These examples are termed 'relevant foods' for the terms of this Guide and are for guidance only. They are subject to the exemptions described in the Temperature Regulations.

Category	Food Types and Examples
a) Dairy products	• Soft or semi-hard cheeses ripened by moulds and/or bacteria. • Dairy-based desserts (including milk substitutes) e.g. fromage frais, mousses, creme caramels, products containing whipped cream.
b) Cooked products	• Food comprising or containing cooked products such as meat, fish, eggs (or meat, fish or egg substitutes), milk, hard and soft cheese, cereals (including rice), pulses and vegetables, whether or not they are intended to be eaten without further reheating, e.g. prepared meals, pies, quiches, flans. • Ready to eat products containing fillings, toppings etc. prepared with the above foods, e.g. sandwiches.
c) Smoked or cured products	• Smoked or cured fish (whether the fish is whole or sliced), e.g. smoked salmon, smoked mackerel. Also, raw scrombroid fish, e.g. tuna, mackerel. • Smoked or cured ready to eat meat which is not stable at ambient temperatures, e.g. sliced, cured cooked meats such as hams, some salamis and other fermented sausages.
d) Prepared ready to eat foods including vegetables	• Prepared vegetables e.g. sliced carrots. • Vegetable salads containing fruit e.g. Waldorf salad. • Prepared salads e.g. coleslaw. • Prepared products e.g. mayonnaise.
e) Uncooked or partly cooked pastry and dough products	• Pizza, sausage rolls. • Fresh pasta containing meat/fish (or substitutes for meat and fish) or vegetables, e.g. uncooked ravioli. • Fresh pasta, whether or not it contains the above foods.

TEMPERATURE CONTROL REQUIREMENTS FOR SCOTLAND

Legal requirement	Guide to compliance	Advice on good practice

Chill and hot holding requirements

13.-(1) *Subject to paragraph (2), no person shall keep food with respect to which any commercial operation is being carried out at or in food premises otherwise than -*

(a) in a refrigerator or refrigerating chamber or in a cool ventilated place; or

(b) at a temperature above 63°C.

This Regulation applies to 'relevant food' (see Table IV, page 64) and requires that it be kept in a refrigerator, cabinet, or in a cool ventilated place, unless it is to be served hot, when it must be kept above 63°C. No chill temperature is specified.

It is good practice to keep all relevant food at or below 8°C. A refrigerator temperature of 5°C or below is recommended.

(2) *Paragraph (1) shall not apply to any food -*

(a) which is undergoing preparation for sale;

(b) which is exposed for sale or has been sold to a consumer whether for immediate consumption or otherwise

(c) which, immediately following any process of cooking to which it is subjected or the final processing stage if no cooking process is applied, is being cooled under hygienic conditions as quickly as possible to a temperature which would not result in a risk to health;

This exempts relevant food from having to be kept cold or above 63°C when:

● it is being prepared for sale;

● is exposed for sale or has been sold to a consumer;

● it is being cooled under hygienic conditions, (i.e. is not exposed to any risk of contamination).

(d) which, in order that it may be conveniently available for sale on the premises to consumers, it is reasonable to keep otherwise than as referred to in paragraph (1);

This applies to food which will be used to replenish displays. This does not need to be kept chilled or above 63°C, where it is reasonable to do so.

Quantities of these foods should be kept to a minimum and should not be kept out of temperature control for excessive periods of time.

Legal requirement	Guide to compliance	Advice on good practice
(e) which, for the duration of its shelf life, may be kept at ambient temperatures with no risk to health;	Some relevant foods are 'shelf stable' and may not require chilled storage. Refer to guidance on regulation 5(b).	
(f) to which Council Regulation (EEC) No. 1906/90 on certain marketing standards for poultry, as amended, applies;	Refer to guidance on regulation 5(f) for the storage of poultry meat.	
(g) to which Council Regulation (EEC) No. 1907/90 on certain marketing standards for eggs, as amended, applies.	Refer to guidance on regulation 5(g) for the storage of eggs.	

Reheating of food

Legal requirement	Guide to compliance	Advice on good practice
14.-(1) Food which in the course of a commercial operation has been heated and which is thereafter reheated before being served for immediate consumption or exposed for sale shall, on being reheated, be raised to a temperature of not less than 82°C.	Reheated foods for service or display must be reheated to at least 82°C. This only applies to food which is reheated in part of the same business where that food was prepared.	Where possible, food should be stirred to ensure an even distribution of heat. A probe thermometer should be used to monitor the internal food temperature. Probes should be disinfected before and after use. Ready meals prepared elsewhere should be reheated to a minimum of 75°C, or to 70°C for 2 minutes.
(2) In any proceedings for an offence under paragraph (1), it shall be a defence for the person charged to prove that he could not have raised the food to a temperature of not less than 82°C without a deterioration of its qualities.	There is an exemption to 14 (1) above where reheating the food to 82°C would result in a deterioration of its quality.	It is good practice to reheat food to a minimum of 75°C or to 70°C for 2 minutes.

Treatment of gelatine

Legal requirement	Guide to compliance	Advice on good practice
15.-(1) Gelatine intended for use in the preparation of bakers' confectionery filling, meat products or fish products in the course of the activities of a food business shall, immediately before use, be brought to the boil or brought to and kept at a temperature of not less than 71°C for 30 minutes.	Before use, gelatine should be brought to the boil **or** brought to, and kept at a minimum of 71°C for at least 30 minutes.	Regular temperature checks should be made during the 30 minute period to ensure the gelatine is being kept at 71°C or above.
(2) Any gelatine left over after the completion of the process shall, if not treated as waste, be cooled under hygienic conditions as quickly as is reasonably practicable and when cold shall be kept in a refrigerator or a refrigerating chamber or a cool ventilated place.	Any gelatine which is left over must either, be treated as waste and disposed of, or cooled under hygienic conditions as quickly as possible and then stored in a refrigerator, refrigerating chamber or cool ventilated place.	Gelatine should preferably be kept in a refrigerator operating at 5°C.

Legal requirement	Guide to compliance	Advice on good practice

Food which is a risk to health

16.-(1) *Subject to paragraphs (2) and (3), no person shall in the course of the activities of a food business keep any products which are -*
(a) raw materials, ingredients, intermediate products or finished products; and

(b) likely to support the growth of pathogenic micro-organisms or the formation of toxins,

at temperatures which would result in a risk to health.

This is a general requirement to keep all foods which are likely to support the growth of pathogenic micro-organisms, or the formation of toxins, at 'safe' temperatures.
For relevant foods - see Table IV, page 64. No temperature is specified.

In most cases, food businesses complying with the more specific requirements in regulations 13 to 15 will also be complying with this regulation.

(2) *Consistent with food safety, limited periods outside temperature control are permitted where necessary to accommodate the practicalities of handling during preparation, transport, storage, display and service of food.*

Relevant food may spend short periods outside of temperature control to accommodate the practicalities of handling during preparation, transport, storage, display and service of food, providing that the time period is consistent with food safety. Every effort must be made to keep this time outside of temperature control as short as possible.

The 'limited period' and permitted temperature variations are not specified by the Temperature Regulations but under normal circumstances, a single limited period of up to two hours outside of temperature control should not be exceeded.

(3) *Paragraph (1) shall not apply to any food which immediately following a final heat processing stage, or a final preparation stage if no heat process is applied, is being cooled as quickly as possible to a temperature which would not result in a risk to health.*

Allowances are made for relevant food which has undergone a final heat processing or preparation stage and is being cooled as quickly as possible to a 'safe' temperature. Food which is in the process of cooling must not be placed so it is at risk of contamination.

It is good practice to allow hot food to cool for no longer than 4 hours before putting it in a cool place, preferably a refrigerator.

Large quantities of food will cool quicker if they are split into smaller portions. See regulation 11, above.

Part 5
TRADERS' CHECKLISTS

Traders' Checklists

The Traders' Checklists are designed to outline the minimum standards required for different types of businesses operating within markets and fairs to comply with the Food Safety (General Food Hygiene) Regulations 1995 and The Food Safety (Temperature Control) Regulations 1995. They cover businesses which operate from permanent or temporary stalls, mobile vehicles and hand carts.

Reference should be made to the main chapters of the Markets and Fairs Industry Guide to Good Hygiene Practice for more detailed information and advice on good practice.

Where traders deal with more than one type of foodstuff, each relevant checklist should be consulted. Where the standards in these checklists vary, the highest standard will be applicable to that business.

Checklists have been produced for the following types of traders:

- Butcher/poulterer/game dealer
- Candyfloss/doughnuts
- Caterer
- Delicatessen
- Fishmonger
- Greengrocer
- Grocer
- Hot Chestnut Seller
- Ice Cream Vendor

If your business is not covered by one of these checklists, or to obtain advice on other ways of complying with the Regulations or Temperature Regulations which may be acceptable - consult your local Environmental Health Officer.

The checklists can be freely copied with the intention that they can be used as a quick and easy source of reference.

BUTCHER/POULTERER/GAME DEALER CHECKLIST

Selling fresh meat only.

If selling raw and cooked meat or other high risk food you will need to apply higher food safety and hygiene standards and should consult the checklist for a delicatessen.

The 'Guide to Compliance' information must be given due consideration by enforcing officers of food authorities when they assess compliance with the Regulations, whereas 'Advice on Good Practice' is simply a recommendation.

The reference column refers to the appropriate page of the Industry Guide to Good Hygiene Practice for Markets and Fairs and to the legislation in the Food Safety (General Food Hygiene) Regulations 1995 and the Food Safety (Temperature Control) Regulations 1995.

Reference should be made to the Glossary of the Industry Guide to Good Hygiene Practice for Markets and Fairs for definitions of terms used in this checklist.

Following the steps below will help to ensure the food you sell from your stall, vehicle or handcart is safe.

Note: The guidance in this checklist may be updated in the light of specific Government legislative proposals implementing the Pennington Group recommendations for the control of E.coli 0157.

Reference	Guide to compliance	Advice on good practice
1. Looking at What You Do	**You must:**	
The Food Safety (General Food Hygiene) Regulations 1995 regulation 4(1)	Carry on your business in a hygienic manner.	
Part 2 regulation 4(3) pages 4-6	Identify the possible problems or hazards that could occur with food in your care (food hazards). Ensure these hazards are controlled and that checks are carried out to ensure the controls are effective.	It is good practice to keep written records of the identified problems, control measures and checks carried out. Examples of possible hazards, their control measures and checks needed for a typical business are given in the table at the end of this checklist.
2. Staff	**You must:**	
Part 3 Chapter X page 46	Ensure all staff handling food (food handlers) receive adequate instruction and supervision to ensure they know how to do their job hygienically.	Instructions should be repeated at suitable intervals or explained as necessary as indicated by the observations of supervision.
Part 3 Chapter VIII 1,2 and regulation 5, pages 39-41	Provide <u>all</u> staff with information about the standards of personal hygiene they have to maintain and what to do if they are suffering from any skin complaints or stomach upsets. Waterproof dressings must be available for covering open cuts/abrasions. Ensure all staff wear suitable, clean clothing. This will be fulfilled by staff handling unwrapped meat wearing clean protective overclothing.	High visibility waterproof plasters are recommended. It is recommended that where meat is likely to come into contact with the head or neck a hat or suitable head covering covers the hair. Protective clothing should preferably cover the arms and body.

Reference	Guide to compliance	Advice on good practice
3. *Care of Food*	**You must:**	
Part 3 *Chapter III,2(h), page 28* *Chapter IX, 1, 2, 3, pages 42-44*	Ensure all meat is fit to eat and is stored correctly to prevent harmful deterioration or contamination. Ensure all areas are kept clean and tidy and free from pests.	
Part 3 *Chapter III, 2(g), page 27* *Chapter IX, 2, page 43* *Part 4* *4, 5(f), 13, pages 53, 56 and 65*	Ensure fresh meat intended to be eaten raw (e.g. steak tartare) is kept at or below 8°C.(England and Wales) or in a refrigerator or cool, ventilated place (Scotland) unless exemptions apply. Ensure fresh poultry meat (chicken, ducks, geese, turkey and guinea fowl) is kept and/or displayed for sale at a temperature not exceeding 4°C or less than -2°C. Ensure frozen poultry meat does not exceed -12°C, or -18°C for quick frozen poultry meat.	It is good practice to keep raw meat chilled to reduce the growth of food spoilage organisms and pathogens and to preserve the quality of the food.
4. *Premises*	**You must:**	
Part 3 *Chapter I, 2, page 9* *Chapter III, 1, page 20*	Ensure the premises are of adequate size to enable safe and hygienic working conditions.	
Part 3 *Chapter I, 7, page 13 and* *Chapter III, 1, page 21*	Ensure adequate lighting (natural/artificial) is provided.	It is recommended that light fittings should be flush mounted, of simple design, corrosion resistant, easily cleaned and designed to prevent broken glass falling onto food.
Part 3 *Chapter I, 5, page 13* *Chapter III, 1, page 21*	Ensure adequate natural or mechanical ventilation is provided.	Reliance upon natural ventilation/market hall ventilation system is likely to be satisfactory in most instances.
Part 3 *Chapter I, 2, page 9* *Chapter III, 1, page 20*	Ensure good layout (in terms of location of storage areas, preparation areas, hand and equipment washing facilities, display area, etc.) to enable the use of good hygiene practices and to make cleaning easy.	

Reference	Guide to compliance	Advice on good practice
Part 3 Chapter I, 1, 2, pages 8, 9 Chapter III, 1, 2(b), (c), (e), pages 20-25. Chapter V, page 33	Ensure the premises, food contact surfaces and equipment are kept clean and maintained in good condition. This will involve regular inspection of your premises to identify any structural defects or broken equipment and the arrangement of necessary remedial action. For acceptable surface finishes see Appendix E of the Industry Guide to Good Hygiene Practice for Markets and Fairs, page 133.	Draw up a routine cleaning schedule to ensure that all parts of the premises are thoroughly cleaned on a regular basis.
5. Access to Facilities	**You must:**	
Part 3 Chapter I, 3, 4, pages 11-13 Chapter III, 2(a), page 22	Ensure facilities for cleaning hands are provided on the premises. On permanent stalls this must be a wash hand basin with hot and cold (or warm) water, soap and a means of drying hands (preferably disposable towels). Mobile/temporary premises may use bowls.	On mobile/temporary premises other hand cleaning facilities are acceptable e.g. commercial quality sanitised handwipes.
Part 3 Chapter II, 2, page 18 Chapter III, 2(c), page 24	Where equipment needs to be washed on the premises to ensure food safety, ensure facilities are provided e.g. sink with hot and cold (or warm) water. Mobile/temporary premises may use bowls. A single facility for equipment and hand washing is acceptable provided these activities can be carried out effectively and without prejudice to food safety.	Any equipment used on mobile or temporary premises may be returned to a base depot for cleaning to reduce the number or size of sinks needed.
6. Water Supply	**You must:**	
Part 3 Chapter III, 2(e), page 25 Chapter VII, 1, page 37	Where washing facilities need to be provided (see above), ensure an adequate supply of potable (drinking) water is provided on the stall/vehicle/handcart, preferably from the mains water supply. Where connection to the mains supply is not possible, water containers may be used. These must be filled from a potable supply. Ensure clean water containers are capable of being cleaned and are cleaned and disinfected regularly.	Clean water containers should be clearly distinguishable from waste water containers.

Reference	Guide to compliance	Advice on good practice
Part 3 Chapter II, 2, page 18	Ensure that where hot water is required there is an adequate potable supply. This can be provided from the main storage system or by an instantaneous gas or electric water heater. Where there are no services to the stall/vehicle/handcart, insulated containers of hot water are acceptable.	
7. Food Contact Surfaces and Equipment (e.g. display areas, cutting boards, mincers, slicing machines, utensils, etc).	**You must:**	
Part 3 Chapter II, 1(f), page 17 Chapter III 1, 2(b), pages 20-24 Chapter V, 1, page 33	Ensure all food contact surfaces and equipment are in good repair, kept clean and have finishes that allow effective cleaning and disinfection. Suitable finishes include stainless steel, ceramics, food grade plastics. Ensure wooden chopping blocks, used for raw meat, are not used when their condition has deteriorated to the point where they cannot be effectively cleaned. Ensure cardboard, waxed paper or other similar disposable containers used for food transport or display are not re-used where there is a risk of contamination in subsequent use.	Correct cleaning of wooden chopping blocks is likely to include scraping to remove surface contamination and cleaning with small amounts of water with a sanitiser.
8. Waste Disposal	**You must:**	
Part 3 Chapter III, 2(f), page 26 Chapter VI, 1, 2, 3, pages 35-36	Ensure all waste is stored so that it does not pose a contamination risk to any food or attract insects/pests. Ensure that where there is no possibility of connection to the mains drainage system via a trapped connection, waste water is stored in an enclosed container and disposed of carefully down a suitable foul water drain, on site or back at a base depot, so as not to cause a risk of contamination to food.	This will normally involve providing a lidded, washable container.

Other ways of complying with the Regulations may be acceptable - consult your local Environmental Health Officer for advice.

BUTCHER/POULTERER/GAME DEALER

FOOD HAZARDS AND THEIR CONTROL

PROCESS Receipt, storage, cutting and serving of fresh meat and poultry.

Note: Supervision, instruction and/or training is applicable at each step.

Step	Hazard	Control Measure	Monitoring	Recommendation
Receipt of food.	Contamination.	Buy from a reputable supplier. Packaging intact and clean.	Check goods on receipt. Inspect packaging for damage.	Check your supplier. Visit their premises if possible, check they are approved premises. (Meat Hygiene Service regional office).
	Growth of food poisoning organisms.	Delivery temperature of 8°C or colder for fresh meat and between -2°C and 4°C for chicken, ducks, geese, turkey and guinea fowl.	Check delivery temperature.	A temperature of 0°C - 2°C is recommended for fresh meat.
Storage.	Contamination.	Keep storage areas clean and in good repair.	Check storage areas and equipment are clean before use and in good repair. Visual checks for contamination.	Use a written cleaning schedule and check list for premises and equipment.
	Growth of food poisoning organisms.	Keep meat chilled. Store fresh chicken, ducks, geese, turkey and guinea fowl between -2°C and 4°C.	Regularly check air temperature of refrigerator.	Keep records of temperature checks.
	Infestation by food pests.	Deny access to pests. Control/eradicate existing infestations.	Check regularly for evidence of infestation.	A pest control contractor may be consulted for advice on prevention and proofing.

Step	Hazard	Control Measure	Monitoring	Recommendation
Cutting/ serving/ display for sale.	Contamination.	Use clean premises and equipment, e.g. mincing machine, band saw, tongs, trays, display units etc.	Check premises and equipment are in good repair and kept clean.	Use a written cleaning schedule and check list for premises and equipment. See Appendix C for an example.
		Good personal hygiene, clean hands, clean protective clothing, etc.	Check staff and protective clothing are clean.	Monitor personal hygiene of food handlers.
			Check that wash hand basin/bowl has hot and cold (or warm) water, soap and drying facilities or there is adequate supply of sanitised handwipes (mobile/temporary premises).	
		Protect from contamination from public.		Provide screening between food on display and the public.
	Growth of food poisoning organisms.	Display for sale at 8°C or colder for fresh meat and -2°C to 4°C for chicken, ducks, geese, turkey and guinea fowl.	Regularly check air temperature of refrigerator	Keep records of temperatures of display units.

CANDYFLOSS/DOUGHNUTS CHECKLIST

Sale of candyfloss and doughnuts.

The 'Guide to Compliance' information must be given due consideration by enforcing officers of food authorities when they assess compliance with the Regulations, whereas 'Advice on Good Practice' is simply a recommendation.

The reference column refers to the appropriate page of the Industry Guide to Good Hygiene Practice for Markets and Fairs and to the legislation in the Food Safety (General Food Hygiene) Regulations 1995 and the Food Safety (Temperature Control) Regulations 1995.

Reference should be made to the Glossary of the Industry Guide to Good Hygiene Practice for Markets and Fairs for definitions of terms used in this checklist.

Following the steps below will help to ensure the food you sell from your stall, vehicle or handcart is safe.

Reference	Guide to compliance	Advice on good practice
1. Looking at What You Do	You must:	
The Food Safety (General Food Hygiene) Regulations 1995 regulation 4(1)	Carry on your business in a hygienic manner.	
Part 2 regulation 4(3) pages 4-6	Identify the possible problems or hazards that could occur with food in your care (food hazards). Ensure these hazards are controlled and that checks are carried out to ensure the controls are effective.	It is good practice to keep written records of the identified problems, control measures and checks carried out. Examples of possible hazards, their control measures and checks needed for a typical business are given in the table at the end of this checklist.
2. Staff	You must:	
Part 3 Chapter X, page 46	Ensure all staff handling food (food handlers) receive adequate instruction and supervision to ensure they know how to do their job hygienically.	Instructions should be repeated at suitable intervals or explained as necessary as indicated by the observations of supervision.
Part 3 Chapter VIII, 1, 2, and regulation 5, pages 39-41	Provide <u>all</u> staff with information about the standards of personal hygiene they have to maintain and what to do if they are suffering from any skin complaints or stomach upsets. Waterproof dressings must be available for covering open cuts/abrasions. Ensure all staff wear suitable clean clothing. This will be fulfilled by: ● staff handling open food - clean, protective overclothing; ● staff handling wrapped food - clean clothing.	High visibility waterproof plasters are recommended. It is recommended that hair is covered with a hat or suitable head covering. Protective clothing should preferably cover the arms and body.

Reference	Guide to compliance	Advice on good practice
3. Care of Food	**You must:**	
Part 3 *Chapter III, 2(h), page 28* *Chapter IX, 1, 2, 3, pages 42-44*	Ensure all ingredients are fit to eat and stored correctly to prevent harmful deterioration or contamination. Ensure all areas are kept clean and tidy and free from pests. Protect ready to eat foods on display, from contamination e.g. by covering or providing a 'sneeze screen'.	It is good practice to ensure all food is used within its 'best before' date.
4. Premises	**You must:**	
Part 3 *Chapter I, 2, page 9* *Chapter III, 1, page 20*	Ensure the premises are of adequate size to enable safe and hygienic working conditions.	
Part 3 *Chapter I, 7, page 13* *Chapter III, 1, page 21*	Ensure adequate lighting (natural/artificial) is provided.	It is recommended that light fittings should be flush mounted, of simple design, corrosion resistant, easily cleaned and designed to prevent broken glass falling onto food.
Part 3 *Chapter I, 5, page 13* *Chapter III, 1, page 21*	Ensure adequate natural or mechanical ventilation is provided. It is recommended that this is in the form of a canopy, connected to a flue with a mechanical extract fan, filters and grease trap over larger doughnut frying appliances.	Reliance upon natural ventilation/market hall ventilation system is likely to be satisfactory in most instances.
Part 3 *Chapter I, 2, page 9* *Chapter III, 1, page 20*	Ensure good layout (in terms of location of storage areas, preparation areas, hand and equipment washing facilities, display area, etc.) to enable the use of good hygiene practices and to make cleaning easy.	
Part 3 *Chapter I, 1, 2, pages 8, 9* *Chapter III, 1, 2(b), (c), (e), pages 20-25* *Chapter V, page 33*	Ensure the premises, food contact surfaces and equipment are kept clean and maintained in good condition. This will involve regular inspection of your premises to identify any structural defects or broken equipment and the arrangement of necessary remedial action. For acceptable surface finishes see Appendix E of the Industry Guide to Good Hygiene Practice for Markets and Fairs, page 133.	Draw up a routine cleaning schedule to ensure that all parts of the premises are thoroughly cleaned on a regular basis.

Reference	Guide to compliance	Advice on good practice
5. Access to Facilities	**You must:**	
Part 3 *Chapter I, 3, 4, pages 11-13* *Chapter III, 2(a), page 22*	Ensure facilities for cleaning hands are available. On permanent stalls this must be a wash hand basin with hot and cold (or warm) water, soap and a means of drying hands (preferably disposable towels), although the use of communal facilities, where available, is acceptable. Mobile/temporary premises may use bowls.	On mobile/temporary premises, other hand cleaning facilities are acceptable (e.g. commercial quality sanitised wipes).
Part 3 *Chapter II, 2, page 18* *Chapter III, 2(c), page 24*	Where equipment needs to be washed on the premises to ensure food safety, ensure facilities are provided e.g. sink with hot and cold (or warm) water. On mobile/temporary premises bowls are acceptable. The equipment and hand washing facilities may be provided by a single facility, provided these activities can be carried out effectively and without prejudice to food safety. The use of communal facilities, where available, is acceptable.	Any equipment used on mobile/temporary premises may be returned to a base depot for cleaning to reduce the size or number of sinks needed.
6. Water Supply	**You must:**	
Part 3 *Chapter III, 2(e), page 25* *Chapter VII, 1, page 37.*	Where washing facilities need to be provided (see above) ensure an adequate supply of potable (drinking) water is provided on the stall/vehicle/handcart, preferably from the mains water supply. Where connection to the mains supply is not possible, containers may be used. These must be filled from a potable supply. Ensure clean water containers are capable of being cleaned and are cleaned and disinfected regularly.	Clean water containers should be clearly distinguishable from waste water containers.

Reference	Guide to compliance	Advice on good practice
Part 3 *Chapter II, 2, page 18*	Ensure that where hot water is required there is an adequate potable supply. This can be provided from the main storage system or by an instantaneous gas or electric water heater. Where there are no services to the stall/vehicle/handcart, insulated containers of hot water are acceptable.	
7. Food Contact Surfaces and Equipment (e.g. work surfaces, utensils, equipment, etc).	**You must:**	
Part 3 *Chapter II, 1(f),page 17* *Chapter III, 1, 2(b), pages* *20-24* *Chapter V, 1, page 33*	Ensure all food contact surfaces and equipment are in good repair, kept clean and have finishes that allow effective cleaning and disinfection. Suitable finishes include stainless steel, ceramics, food grade plastics. Ensure cardboard, waxed paper or other similar disposable containers used for food transport or display are not re-used where there is a risk of contamination in subsequent use.	
8. Waste Disposal	**You must:**	
Part 3 *Chapter III, 2(f), page 26* *Chapter VI, 1, 2, 3, pages* *35-36.*	Ensure all waste is stored so that it does not pose a contamination risk to any food or attract insects/pests. Ensure that where there is no possibility of connection to the mains drainage system via a trapped connection, waste water is stored in an enclosed container and disposed of carefully down a suitable foul water drain, on site or back at a base depot, so as not to cause a risk of contamination to food.	This will normally involve providing a lidded, washable container.

Other ways of complying with the Regulations may be acceptable - consult your local Environmental Health Officer for advice.

CANDYFLOSS/DOUGHNUT

FOOD HAZARDS AND THEIR CONTROL

PROCESS Receipt, storage and preparation of candyfloss and doughnuts.

Note: Supervision, instruction and/or training is applicable at each step.

Step	Hazard	Control Measure	Monitoring	Recommendation
Receipt and storage of food.	Contamination. Growth of food poisoning organisms. Infestation by food pests.	Buy from a reputable supplier. Packaging intact and clean. Deny access to pests. Control/eradicate existing infestations.	Check goods on receipt. Inspect packaging for damage. Check regularly for evidence of infestation.	Check your supplier, visit their premises if possible. Check "best before" date. A pest control contractor may be consulted for advice on prevention and proofing.
Preparation/ serving and display for sale.	Contamination.	Premises and equipment kept clean and in good repair. Good personal hygiene, clean hands, clean clothing, etc. Protect from contamination from public.	Check premises and equipment are clean and in good repair. Visual checks for contamination. Check staff and clothing are clean. Check that wash hand basin/bowl has hot and cold (or warm) water, soap and drying facilities or there is an adequate supply of sanitised handwipes (mobile/temporary premises).	Use a written cleaning schedule and check list for premises and equipment. See Appendix C for an example. Provide screening or cover for food on display.

CATERER CHECKLIST

Includes restaurants, cafes, sandwich bars and hot food take-aways.

The 'Guide to Compliance' information must be given due consideration by enforcing officers of food authorities when they assess compliance with the Regulations, whereas 'Advice on Good Practice' is simply a recommendation.

The reference column refers to the appropriate page of the Industry Guide to Good Hygiene Practice for Markets and Fairs and to the legislation in the Food Safety (General Food Hygiene) Regulations 1995 and the Food Safety (Temperature Control) Regulations 1995.

Reference should be made to the Glossary of the Industry Guide to Good Hygiene Practice for Markets and Fairs for definitions of terms used in this checklist.

Following the steps below will help to ensure the food you sell from your stall, vehicle or handcart is safe.

Legal requirement	Guide to compliance	Advice on good practice
1. Looking at What You Do	You must:	
The Food Safety (General Food Hygiene) Regulations 1995 regulation 4(1)	Carry on your business in a hygienic manner.	
Part 2 regulation 4(3) pages 4-6	Identify the possible problems or hazards that could occur with food in your care (food hazards). Ensure these hazards are controlled and that checks are carried out to ensure the controls are effective.	It is good practice to keep written records of the identified problems, control measures and checks carried out. Examples of possible hazards, their control measures and checks needed for a typical business are given in the table at the end of this checklist.
2. Staff	You must:	
Part 3 Chapter X page 46	Ensure all staff handling food (food handlers) receive adequate instruction and supervision to ensure they know how to do their job hygienically. Structured food hygiene training must be undertaken by all staff handling high risk open food, including supervisors/ managers and yourself as the owner of the food business.	Instructions should be repeated at suitable intervals or explained as necessary, as indicated by the observations of supervision. Circumstances should be regularly assessed to highlight the need for training, including refresher training.
Part 3 Chapter VIII 1,2 and regulation 5, pages 39-41	Provide <u>all</u> staff with information about the standards of personal hygiene they have to maintain and what to do if they are suffering from any skin complaints or stomach upsets. Waterproof dressings must be available for covering open cuts/abrasions. Ensure suitable, clean clothing is worn by all staff handling open high risk food. This will be fulfilled by clean protective overclothing and a head covering to contain the hair.	High visibility waterproof plasters are recommended. Protective clothing should preferably cover the arms and body.

Legal requirement	Guide to compliance	Advice on good practice
3. Care of Food	**You must:**	
Part 3 *Chapter III, 2(h),* *page 28* *Chapter IX, 1,2,3 pages 42-44*	Ensure all food is within its 'use by' date, is fit to eat and is stored correctly to prevent harmful deterioration or contamination. Ensure all areas are kept clean and tidy and free from pests.	It is good practice to ensure all food is used within its 'best before' date. Keep a record of the 'use by' date when packaging is removed.
Part 3 *Chapter III, 2(g), page 27* *Chapter IX, 2, page 43* *Part 4* *4, 8, 13, pages 53, 59 and 65*	Keep hot foods at 63°C or hotter, unless exemptions apply. Keep high risk foods which are to be served cold at 8°C or colder (England and Wales), or in a refrigerator or cool ventilated place (Scotland), unless exemptions apply.	It is good practice to keep the refrigerator at 5°C to allow a margin of error.
Part 3 *Chapter II, 2, page 18* *Chapter III,* *paragraph 2(c), (h), pages 24 and 28* *Chapter IX, 2, 3, page 43*	Ensure ready to eat foods are protected from contamination by raw foods e.g. by separation. Use separate chopping boards and slicing equipment for raw foods and ready to eat foods or disinfect between uses. Use separate tongs etc. for service or disinfect between uses. Protect ready to eat foods on display from contamination e.g. by covering or providing a 'sneeze screen'.	
4. Premises	**You must:**	
Part 3 *Chapter I, 2, page 9* *Chapter III, 1, page 20*	Ensure the premises are of adequate size to enable safe and hygienic working conditions.	
Part 3 *Chapter I, 7, page 13* *Chapter III, 1, page 21*	Ensure adequate lighting (natural/artificial) is provided.	It is recommended that light fittings should be flush mounted, of simple design, corrosion resistant, easily cleaned and designed to prevent broken glass falling onto food.
Part 3 *Chapter I, 5, page 13* *Chapter III, 1, page 21*	Ensure adequate natural or mechanical ventilation is provided. It is recommended that a suitable canopy is provided, connected to a flue with a mechanical extract fan, filters and grease trap above any cooking or frying range.	

Legal requirement	Guide to compliance	Advice on good practice
Part 3 *Chapter I, 2, page 9* *Chapter III, 1, page 20*	Ensure good layout (in terms of location of storage areas, preparation areas, hand and equipment washing facilities, display area, etc.) to enable the use of good hygiene practices and to make cleaning easy.	
Part 3 *Chapter I, 1, 2, pages 8, 9* *Chapter III, 1, 2(b), (c), (e), pages 20-25* *Chapter V, page 33*	Ensure the premises, food contact surfaces and equipment are kept clean and maintained in good condition. Food contact surfaces must be capable of being disinfected. This will include regular inspection of your premises to identify any structural defects or broken equipment and the arrangement of necessary remedial action. For acceptable surface finishes see Appendix E of the Industry Guide to Good Hygiene Practice for Markets and Fairs, page 133.	Draw up a routine cleaning schedule to ensure that all parts of the premises are thoroughly cleaned on a regular basis.
5. Access to Facilities	**You must:**	
Part 3 *Chapter I, 3, 4, pages 11-13* *Chapter III, 2(a), page 22*	Ensure facilities for cleaning hands are provided on the stall/vehicle/handcart. On permanent stalls this must be a wash hand basin with soap and a means of drying hands (preferably disposable towels). Mobile/temporary premises may use bowls.	
Part 3 *Chapter II, 2, page 18* *Chapter III, 2(c), page 24*	Where equipment needs to be washed on the premises to ensure food safety, ensure facilities are provided e.g. sink with hot and cold (or warm) water. On mobile/temporary premises bowls are acceptable. The equipment and hand washing facilities must be separate.	Any equipment used on mobile or temporary premises may be returned to a base depot for cleaning to reduce the number or size of sinks needed.
Part 3 *Chapter II, 3, page 18* *Chapter III, 2(d), page 25*	Where food needs to be washed on the premises, ensure facilities are provided e.g. sink with cold and/or hot water. On mobile/temporary premises bowls are acceptable. For small operators, one sink may be acceptable for washing both food and equipment, provided both activities can be done effectively and without prejudice to food safety.	

Legal requirement	Guide to compliance	Advice on good practice
6. Water Supply	**You must:**	
Part 3 *Chapter III, 2 (e), page 25* *Chapter VII, 1, page 37*	Ensure an adequate supply of potable (drinking) water is provided on the stall/vehicle/handcart, preferably from the mains water supply. Where connection to the mains supply is not possible, containers may be used. These must be filled from a potable supply. Ensure clean water containers are capable of being cleaned and are cleaned and disinfected regularly.	Clean water containers should be clearly distinguishable from waste water containers.
Part 3 *Chapter II, 2, page 18*	Ensure an adequate supply of potable hot water. This can be provided from the main storage system, or by an instantaneous gas or electric water heater. Where there are no services to the stall/vehicle/handcart, insulated containers of hot water are acceptable.	
Part 3 *Chapter I, 4, page 12*	It is recommended that hot and cold water are piped to the washing facilities.	
7. Food Contact Surfaces and Equipment **(e.g. display areas serveries, cutting boards, preparation tables, slicing machines, mixers, fridges, freezers, utensils, etc).**	**You must:**	
Part 3 *Chapter II, 1(f),page 17* *Chapter III, 1, 2(b), pages 20-24* *Chapter V, 1, page 33*	Ensure all food contact surfaces and equipment are in good repair, kept clean, and have finishes that allow effective cleaning and disinfection. Suitable finishes include stainless steel, ceramics, food grade plastics. Ensure wooden chopping blocks are not used for the preparation of high risk foods (e.g. cooked meats). Ensure cardboard, waxed paper or other similar disposable containers used for food transport or display are not reused where there is a risk of contamination in subsequent use.	

Legal requirement	Guide to compliance	Advice on good practice
8. Waste Disposal	You must:	
Part 3 *Chapter III, 2(f), page 26* *Chapter VI, 1, 2, 3, pages 35-36*	Ensure all waste is stored so that it does not pose a contamination risk to any food or attract insects/pests. Ensure that where there is no possibility of connection to the mains drainage system via a trapped connection, waste water is stored in an enclosed container and disposed of carefully down a suitable foul water drain, on site or back at a base depot, so as not to cause a risk of contamination to food.	This will normally involve providing a lidded, washable container. The bin lid should preferably not be hand operated.

Other ways of complying with the Regulations may be acceptable - consult your local Environmental Health Officer for advice.

CATERERS

FOOD HAZARDS AND THEIR CONTROL

PROCESS Receipt, storage, preparation, cooking, cooling, reheating and service of hot and cold foods.

Note: Supervision, instruction and/or training is applicable at each step.

Step	Hazard	Control Measure	Monitoring	Recommendation
Receipt and storage.	Contamination.	Buy from a reputable supplier.	Check goods on receipt.	Check your supplier. Visit their premises if possible.
		Packaging intact and clean.	Inspect packaging for damage.	
		Keep premises and equipment clean and in good repair.	Check storage areas and equipment are clean before use and in good repair.	Use a written cleaning schedule and checklist for premises and equipment. See Appendix C for an example.
	Growth of food poisoning organisms.	Keep stored foods wrapped/covered.	Check foods are wrapped/covered.	
		Delivery and storage temperature of high risk food of 8°C or colder.	Check delivery temperature - the air temperature of the vehicle or 'between pack' temperature of products.	Keep records of temperature checks. See Appendix B for a sample record sheet.
			Regularly check air temperature of refrigerator.	
		Use before 'use by' date - rotate stock, buy within 'use by' date.	Check goods on receipt. Daily check of 'use by' dates.	It is good practice to ensure food is sold/used within its 'best before' date.
	Cross contamination.	Separate raw and cooked foods.	Check separation of raw/cooked foods.	
	Infestation by food pests.	Deny access to pests. Control/eradicate existing infestations.	Check regularly for evidence of infestation.	A pest control contractor may be consulted for advice on prevention and proofing.
Preparation.	Contamination.	Good personal hygiene e.g. clean hands, clean protective clothing.	Check staff and protective clothing are clean.	Draw up a code of personal hygiene standards for staff to follow.
			Check that wash hand basin/bowl has hot and cold (or warm) water, soap and drying facilities.	

Step	Hazard	Control Measure	Monitoring	Recommendation
		Keep premises and equipment clean and in good repair.	Check premises and equipment are clean and in good repair. Visual checks for contamination.	Use a written cleaning schedule and checklist for premises and equipment.
	Growth of food poisoning organisms.	Limit time at kitchen temperatures (i.e. return food to refrigerator or cook as soon as possible).	Check food handling practices and preparation times regularly.	
	Cross contamination.	Separate raw and cooked foods. Use separate equipment for ready to eat foods or disinfect between uses.	Check separation of raw/cooked foods, correct use of separate equipment or disinfection between uses.	Use colour coded equipment for raw and cooked food.
Cooking.	Survival of food poisoning bacteria.	Thoroughly defrost frozen foods.	Check foods are defrosted before cooking.	
		Cook foods thoroughly. An internal temperature of 75°C is recommended.	Check internal temperatures of food using a probe thermometer.	Keep records of temperature checks.
		Stir liquid food regularly.	Check stirring is carried out.	
		Avoid bulk preparation.		
	Contamination.	Use clean equipment.	Check equipment is clean.	
Cooling.	Growth of surviving bacteria and/or spores.	Cool food as quickly as possible. When cool, store in a refrigerator at 8°C or below.	Check time and temperature to ensure food is refrigerated as soon as possible.	Reduce cooling periods by: ● reducing joint size (ideally below 3kg.); ● use wide, shallow trays/ containers; ● immerse containers in clean, cold water.
	Further contamination.	Cover foods during cooling and storage where possible.	Check foods are covered.	
		Use clean equipment.	Check equipment is clean.	
	Cross contamination.	Separate raw and cooked foods.	Check separation of raw/cooked foods.	Transfer foods to refrigerator within 1 1/2 hours to chill below 8°C.
				Keep records of temperature checks.

Step	Hazard	Control Measure	Monitoring	Recommendation
Hot holding.	Growth of bacteria.	Keep food above 63°C.	Check internal temperatures of food using a probe thermometer.	Keep records of times and temperature checks.
	Further contamination.	Use clean equipment.	Check equipment is clean.	
		Keep food covered where possible.	Check food is covered.	
Chilled storage.	Growth of bacteria.	Keep food at or below 8°C.	Check refrigeration temperatures.	Keep records of temperature checks.
		Use foods within 'use by' date.	Check 'use by' dates.	Date code high risk, ready to eat foods produced on site.
	Further contamination.	Keep foods wrapped/covered.	Visual checks for contamination.	
		Separate raw/cooked foods.	Check separation of raw/cooked foods.	
		Use clean refrigerators.	Check refrigerators are clean.	
Reheating.	Survival of bacteria.	Reheat to above 75°C (82°C in Scotland).	Check internal food temperatures using a probe thermometer.	Keep written records of temperature checks
		Stir liquid foods to ensure even distribution of heat.		Keep reheating of food to a minimum.
	Further contamination.	Use clean equipment.	Check equipment is clean.	
		Keep food covered where possible.	Check foods are covered. Visual checks for contamination.	

Step	Hazard	Control Measure	Monitoring	Recommendation
Service/ Display.	Growth of bacteria.	Serve high risk hot and cold foods as soon as possible. Keep hot food above 63°C unless displayed for less than 2 hours. Keep chilled food at or below 8°C unless displayed for less than 4 hours.	Regularly check time and temperatures of food.	Keep written records of temperature checks.
	Further contamination.	Use clean equipment. Protect from contamination from public e.g. screen.	Check equipment is clean. Visual checks for contamination. Check screening or wrapping of food on display.	

DELICATESSEN CHECKLIST

Selling unwrapped cooked meats, pies, quiches, cheeses, uncooked foods.

The 'Guide to Compliance' information must be given due consideration by enforcing officers of food authorities when they assess compliance with the Regulations, whereas 'Advice on Good Practice' is simply a recommendation.

The reference column refers to the appropriate page of the Industry Guide to Good Hygiene Practice for Markets and Fairs and to the legislation in the Food Safety (General Food Hygiene) Regulations 1995 and the Food Safety (Temperature Control) Regulations 1995.

Reference should be made to the Glossary of the Industry Guide to Good Hygiene Practice for Markets and Fairs for definitions of terms used in this checklist.

Following the steps below will help to ensure the food you sell from your stall, vehicle or handcart is safe.

Reference	Guide to compliance	Advice on good practice
1. Looking at What You Do	**You must:**	
The Food Safety (General Food Hygiene) Regulations 1995 regulation 4(1)	Carry on your business in a hygienic manner.	
Part 2 regulation 4(3) pages 4-6	Identify the possible problems or hazards that could occur with food in your care (food hazards).	It is good practice to keep written records of the identified problems, control measures and checks carried out.
	Ensure these hazards are controlled and that checks are carried out to ensure the controls are effective.	Examples of possible hazards, their control measures and checks needed for a typical business are given in the table at the end of this checklist.
2. Staff	**You must:**	
Part 3 Chapter X, page 46	Ensure all staff handling food (food handlers) receive adequate instruction and supervision to ensure they know how to do their job hygienically.	Instructions should be repeated at suitable intervals or explained as necessary, as indicated by the observations of supervision.
	Structured food hygiene training must be undertaken by all staff handling high risk open food, including supervisors/ managers and yourself as the owner of the food business.	Circumstances should be regularly assessed to highlight the need for training, including refresher training.
Part 3 Chapter VIII, 1, 2 and regulation 5, pages 39-41	Provide all staff with information about the standards of personal hygiene they have to maintain and what to do if they are suffering from any skin complaints or stomach upsets. Waterproof dressings must be available for covering open cuts/abrasions.	High visibility waterproof plasters are recommended.
	Ensure suitable, clean clothing is worn by all staff handling open high risk food. This will be fulfilled by clean protective overclothing and a head covering to contain the hair.	Protective clothing should preferably cover the arms and body.

Reference	Guide to compliance	Advice on good practice
3. Care of Food	**You must:**	
Part 3 *Chapter III, 2(h), page 28* *Chapter IX, 1, 2, 3, pages 42-44*	Ensure all food is within its 'use by' date, is fit to eat, and is stored correctly to prevent harmful deterioration or contamination. Ensure all areas are kept clean and tidy and free from pests.	It is good practice to ensure all food is sold within its 'best before' date. Keep a record of the 'use by' date when the packaging is removed. It is helpful to the consumer if the 'use by' and 'best before' dates are prominently displayed.
Part 3 *Chapter III, 2(g), page 27* *Chapter IX, 2, page 43* *Part 4* *4,13, pages 53 & 65*	Keep cooked meats and other high risk foods at 8°C or colder (England and Wales) or in a refrigerator or a cool ventilated place (Scotland) unless exemptions apply.	It is good practice to keep the refrigerator at 5°C to allow a margin of error.
Part 3 *Chapter II, 2, page 18* *Chapter III, 2(c), (h), pages 24 & 28* *Chapter IX, 2,3, page 43*	Ensure ready to eat foods are protected from contamination by raw foods e.g. by separation. Use separate chopping boards and slicing equipment for raw foods and ready to eat foods or disinfect between uses. Use separate tongs etc. for service or disinfect between uses. Protect ready to eat foods on display from contamination e.g. by covering or providing a 'sneeze screen'.	
4. Premises	**You must:**	
Part 3 *Chapter I, 2, page 9* *Chapter III, 1, page 20*	Ensure the premises are of adequate size to enable safe and hygienic working conditions.	
Part 3 *Chapter I, 7, page 13* *Chapter III, 1, page 21*	Ensure adequate lighting (natural/ artificial) is provided.	It is recommended that light fittings should be flush mounted, of simple design, corrosion resistant, easily cleaned and designed to prevent broken glass falling onto food.
Part 3 *Chapter I, 5, page 13* *Chapter III, 1, page 21*	Ensure adequate natural or mechanical ventilation is provided.	Reliance upon natural ventilation/market hall ventilation system is likely to be satisfactory in most instances.
Part 3 *Chapter I, 2, page 9* *Chapter III, 1, page 20*	Ensure good layout (in terms of location of storage areas, preparation areas, hand and equipment washing facilities, display area, etc.) to enable the use of good hygiene practices and to make cleaning easy.	

Reference	Guide to compliance	Advice on good practice
Part 3 *Chapter I, 1, 2, pages 8, 9* *Chapter III, 1, 2(b), (c), (e), pages 20-25* *Chapter V, page 33*	Ensure the premises, food contact surfaces and equipment are kept clean and maintained in good condition. Food contact surfaces must be capable of being disinfected. This will involve regular inspection of your premises to identify any structural defects or broken equipment and the arrangement of necessary remedial action. For acceptable surface finishes see Appendix E of the Industry Guide to Good Hygiene Practice for Markets and Fairs, page 133.	Draw up a routine cleaning schedule to ensure that all parts of the premises are thoroughly cleaned on a regular basis.
5. Access to Facilities	**You must:**	
Part 3 *Chapter I, 3, 4, pages 11-13* *Chapter III, 2(a), page 22*	Ensure facilities for cleaning hands are provided on the stall/vehicle/handcart. On permanent stalls this must be a wash hand basin with hot and cold (or warm) water, soap and a means of drying hands (preferably disposable towels). Mobile/temporary premises may use bowls.	
Part 3 *Chapter II, 2, page 18* *Chapter III, 2(c), page 24*	Where equipment needs to be washed on the premises to ensure food safety, ensure facilities are provided e.g. sink with hot and cold (or warm) water. On mobile/temporary premises, bowls are acceptable. The equipment and hand washing facilities must be separate.	Any equipment used on mobile/temporary premises may be returned to a base depot for cleaning to reduce the size or number of sinks needed.
6. Water Supply	**You must:**	
Part 3 *Chapter III, 2(e), page 25* *Chapter VII, 1, page 37*	Ensure an adequate supply of potable (drinking) water is provided on the stall/vehicle/handcart, preferably from the mains water supply. Where connection to the mains supply is not possible, containers may be used. These must be filled from a potable supply. Ensure clean water containers are capable of being cleaned and are cleaned and disinfected regularly.	Clean water containers should be clearly distinguishable from waste water containers.

Reference	Guide to compliance	Advice on good practice
Part 3 *Chapter II, 2, page 18*	Ensure an adequate supply of potable hot water. This can be provided from the main storage system or by an instantaneous gas or electric water heater. Where there are no services to the stall/vehicle/handcart, insulated containers of hot water are acceptable.	
Part 3 *Chapter I, 4, page 12*	It is recommended that hot and cold water are piped to the washing facilities.	
7. *Food Contact Surfaces and Equipment (e.g. display areas, cutting boards, slicing machines, utensils, etc).*	You must:	
Part 3 *Chapter II, 1(f), page 17* *Chapter III, 1, 2(b), pages 20-24* *Chapter V, 1, page 33*	Ensure all food contact surfaces and equipment are in good repair, kept clean and have finishes that allow effective cleaning and disinfection. Suitable finishes include stainless steel, ceramics, food grade plastics. Ensure wooden chopping blocks are not used for the preparation of high risk foods (e.g. cooked meats). Ensure cardboard, waxed paper or other similar disposable containers used for food transport or display are not re-used where there is a risk of contamination in subsequent use.	
8. *Waste Disposal*	You must:	
Part 3 *Chapter III, 2 (f), page 26* *Chapter VI, 1, 2, 3, pages 35-36*	Ensure all waste is stored so that it does not pose a contamination risk or attract insects/pests. Ensure that where there is no possibility of connection to the mains drainage system via a trapped connection, waste water is stored in an enclosed container and disposed of carefully down a suitable foul water drain, on site or back at a base depot, so as not to cause a risk of contamination to food.	This will normally involve providing a lidded, washable container. The bin lid should preferably not be hand operated.

Other ways of complying with the Regulations may be acceptable - consult your local Environmental Health Officer for advice.

DELICATESSEN

FOOD HAZARDS AND THEIR CONTROL

PROCESS Receipt, storage, slicing, display and service of ready to eat and uncooked foods.

Note: Supervision, instruction and/or training is applicable at each step.

Step	Hazard	Control Measure	Monitoring	Recommendation
Receipt of food.	Contamination.	Buy from a reputable supplier.	Check goods on receipt.	Check your supplier's premises if possible.
		Packaging intact and clean.	Inspect packaging for damage.	
	Growth of food poisoning organisms.	Within 'use by' date.	Check food within 'use by' date.	Check food is within its 'best before' date.
		Delivery temperature of 8°C or colder.	Check delivery temperature - the air temperature of the vehicle or 'between pack' temperature of products.	Keep records of temperature checks. See Appendix B for a sample record sheet.
Storage.	Cross contamination.	Keep cooked and raw food separate.	Visual daily checks to ensure adequate separation of raw/cooked food.	
	Contamination.	Premises and equipment kept clean and in good repair.	Check storage areas are clean and in good repair.	Use a written cleaning schedule and check list for premises and equipment. See Appendix C for an example.
		Keep stored foods wrapped/covered.	Check foods are wrapped/covered.	
	Growth of food poisoning organisms.	Store at 8°C or colder.	Regularly check air temperature of refrigerator.	Keep records of temperature checks.
		Rotate stock. Use before 'use by' date.	Daily check 'use by' dates.	It is good practice to ensure food is sold within its 'best before' date.
	Infestation by food pests.	Deny access to pests. Control and eradicate existing infestations.	Check regularly for evidence of infestation.	A pest control contractor may be consulted for advice on prevention and proofing.

Step	Hazard	Control Measure	Monitoring	Recommendation
Food preparation including slicing and serving.	Contamination.	Premises and equipment kept clean and in good repair.	Inspect premises and equipment to ensure it is clean and in good repair.	Use a written cleaning schedule and check list for premises and equipment. See Appendix C for an example.
		Use separate equipment for raw and cooked foods or disinfect between uses.	Check use of separate equipment and/or adequate disinfection.	Use colour-coded equipment for raw and cooked food.
		Good personal hygiene, e.g. clean hands, clean protective clothing.	Check staff and protective clothing are clean.	
			Check that wash hand basin/bowl has hot and cold (or warm) water, soap and drying facilities.	
	Growth of food poisoning organisms.	Return joint to refrigeration after slicing - do not leave on machine.		
		Use before 'use by' date.	Retain wrapping of food where 'use by' date is printed or make a note of it.	Check 'best before' dates.
Display for sale.	Contamination.	Separate raw and cooked foods.	Visual daily checks to ensure raw and cooked foods are adequately separated.	
		Use clean trays and display units.	Inspect/check equipment before use to ensure it is clean.	
		Protect food from contamination from public.	Check screening/ wrapping of food on display.	
	Growth of food poisoning organisms.	Keep high risk food at 8°C or colder unless displayed for less than 4 hours.	Regularly check fridge/ food temperature.	Keep records of temperature checks carried out.

FISHMONGER CHECKLIST

Selling fresh fish only.

If selling raw and cooked fish or other high risk food you will need to apply higher food safety and hygiene standards and should consult the checklist for a delicatessen.

The 'Guide to Compliance' information must be given due consideration by enforcing officers of food authorities when they assess compliance with the Regulations, whereas 'Advice on Good Practice' is simply a recommendation.

The reference column refers to the appropriate page of the Industry Guide to Good Hygiene Practice for Markets and Fairs and to the legislation in the Food Safety (General Food Hygiene) Regulations 1995 and the Food Safety (Temperature Control) Regulations 1995.

Reference should be made to the Glossary of the Industry Guide to Good Hygiene Practice for Markets and Fairs for definitions of terms used in this checklist.

Following the steps below will help to ensure the food you sell from your stall, vehicle or handcart is safe.

Reference	Guide to compliance	Advice on good practice
1. Looking at What You Do	**You must:**	
The Food Safety (General Food Hygiene) Regulations 1995 regulation 4(1)	Carry on your business in a hygienic manner.	
Part 2 regulation 4(3) pages 4-6	Identify the possible problems or hazards that could occur with food in your care (food hazards). Ensure these hazards are controlled and that checks are carried out to ensure the controls are effective.	It is good practice to keep written records of the identified problems, control measures and checks carried out. Examples of possible hazards, their control measures and checks needed for a typical business are given in the table at the end of this checklist.
2. Staff	**You must:**	
Part 3 Chapter X, page 46	Ensure all staff handling food (food handlers) receive adequate instruction and supervision to ensure they know how to do their job hygienically.	Instructions should be repeated at suitable intervals or explained as necessary, as indicated by the observations of supervision.
Part 3 Chapter VIII, 1, 2 and regulation 5, pages 39-41	Provide <u>all</u> staff with information about the standards of personal hygiene they have to maintain and what to do if they are suffering from any skin complaints or stomach upsets. Waterproof dressings must be available for covering open cuts/abrasions. Ensure all staff wear suitable, clean clothing. This will be fulfilled by staff handling unwrapped fish wearing clean protective overclothing.	High visibility waterproof plasters are recommended. It is recommended that hair is covered with a hat or suitable head cover. Protective clothing should preferably cover the arms and body.

Reference	Guide to compliance	Advice on good practice
3. Care of Food	**You must:**	
Part 3 *Chapter III, 2(h), page 28* *Chapter IX, 1, 2, 3, pages 42-44*	Ensure all fish on the stall/vehicle/handcart is fit to eat and is stored correctly to prevent harmful deterioration or contamination. Ensure all areas are kept clean and tidy and free from pests.	
Part 3 *Chapter III, 2(g), page 27* *Chapter IX, 2, page 43* *Part 4* *4, 13, pages 53 and 65*	Ensure raw scrombroid fish (e.g. tuna and mackerel) and fish intended to be eaten raw, e.g. sushi, is kept at or below 8°C (in England and Wales) or in a refrigerator or cool ventilated place (Scotland) unless exemptions apply.	All chilled fish should be maintained at a temperature as close to 0°C as possible to preserve its quality. Icing is the best means of chilling fish.
4. Premises	**You must:**	
Part 3 *Chapter I, 2, page 9* *Chapter III, 1, page 20*	Ensure the premises are of adequate size to enable safe and hygienic working conditions.	
Part 3 *Chapter I, 7, page 13* *Chapter III, 1, page 21*	Ensure adequate lighting (natural/artificial) is provided.	It is recommended that light fittings should be flush mounted, of simple design, corrosion resistant, easily cleaned and designed to prevent broken glass falling onto food.
Part 3 *Chapter I, 5, page 13* *Chapter III, 1, page 21*	Ensure adequate natural or mechanical ventilation is provided.	Reliance upon natural ventilation/market hall ventilation system is likely to be satisfactory in most instances.
Part 3 *Chapter I, 2, page 9* *Chapter III, 1, page 20*	Ensure good layout (in terms of location of storage areas, preparation areas, hand and equipment washing facilities, display area, etc.) to enable the use of good hygiene practices and to make cleaning easy.	
Part 3 *Chapter I, 1, 2, pages 8, 9* *Chapter III, 1, 2(b) (c) (e), pages 20-25* *Chapter V, page 33*	Ensure the stall/vehicle/handcart, food contact surfaces and equipment are kept clean and maintained in good condition. This will involve regular inspection of your stall/vehicle/handcart to identify any structural defects or broken equipment and the arrangement of any necessary remedial action. For acceptable surface finishes see Appendix E of the Industry Guide to Good Hygiene Practice for Markets and Fairs, page 133.	Draw up a routine cleaning schedule to ensure that all parts of the premises are thoroughly cleaned on a regular basis.

Reference	Guide to compliance	Advice on good practice
5. Access to Facilities	**You must:**	
Part 3 *Chapter I, 3, 4, pages 11-13* *Chapter III, 2(a), page 22*	Ensure facilities for cleaning hands are provided on the premises. On permanent stalls this must be a wash hand basin with hot and cold (or warm) water, soap and a means of drying hands (preferably disposable towels). Mobile/temporary premises may use bowls.	On mobile/temporary premises other hand cleaning facilities are acceptable e.g. commercial quality sanitised handwipes.
Part 3 *Chapter II, 2, page 18* *Chapter III, 2(c), page 24*	Where equipment needs to be washed on the premises to ensure food safety, ensure facilities are provided e.g. sink with hot and cold (or warm) water. Mobile/temporary premises may use bowls.	Any equipment used on mobile or temporary premises may be returned to a base depot for cleaning to reduce the number or size of sinks needed.
Part 3 *Chapter II, 3, page 18* *Chapter III, 2(d), page 25*	Where food needs to be washed on the premises, ensure facilities are provided e.g. sink with cold water. On mobile/ temporary premises bowls are acceptable. A single facility for equipment, food and hand washing is acceptable, provided these activities can be carried out effectively and without prejudice to food safety.	
6. Water Supply	**You must:**	
Part 3 *Chapter III, 2(e), page 25* *Chapter VII, 1, page 37*	Where washing facilities need to be provided (see above), ensure an adequate supply of potable (drinking) water is provided on the stall/vehicle/handcart, preferably from the mains water supply. Where connection to the mains supply is not possible, water containers may be used. These must be filled from a potable supply. Ensure clean water containers are capable of being cleaned and are cleaned and disinfected regularly.	Clean water containers should be clearly distinguishable from waste water containers.
Part 3 *Chapter II, 2, page 18*	Ensure that where hot water is required there is an adequate potable supply. This can be provided from the main storage system or by an instantaneous gas or electric water heater. Where there are no services to the stall/vehicle/handcart, insulated containers of hot water are acceptable.	

Reference	Guide to compliance	Advice on good practice
Part 3 *Chapter I, 4, page 12*	It is recommended that hot and cold water is piped to the wash hand basin/sink.	
7. Food Contact Surfaces and Equipment **(e.g. display areas, cutting boards, scales, utensils, etc).**	**You must:**	
Part 3 *Chapter II, 1(f),page 17* *Chapter III 1, 2(b),pages 20-24* *Chapter V, 1, page 33*	Ensure all food contact surfaces and equipment are in good repair and kept clean and have finishes that allow effective cleaning and disinfection. Suitable finishes include stainless steel, ceramics, food grade plastics. Ensure wooden chopping blocks, used for raw fish, are not used when their condition has deteriorated to the point where they cannot be effectively cleaned. Ensure cardboard, waxed paper or other similar disposable containers used for food transport or display are not re-used where there is a risk of contamination in subsequent use.	Correct cleaning of wooden chopping blocks is likely to include, scraping to remove surface contamination and cleaning with small amounts of water with a sanitiser.
8. Waste Disposal	**You must:**	
Part 3 *Chapter III, 2(f), page 26* *Chapter VI, 1, 2, 3, pages 35-36*	Ensure all waste is stored so that it does not pose a contamination risk to any food or attract insects/pests. Ensure that where there is no possibility of connection to the mains drainage system via a trapped connection, waste water is stored in an enclosed container and disposed of carefully down a suitable foul water drain, on site or back at a base depot, so as not to cause a risk of contamination to food.	This will normally involve providing a lidded, washable container.

Other ways of complying with the Regulations may be acceptable - consult your local Environmental Health Officer for advice.

FISHMONGER

FOOD HAZARDS AND THEIR CONTROL

PROCESS Receipt, storage and sale of wet fish.

Note: Supervision, instruction and/or training is applicable at each step.

Step	Hazard	Control Measure	Monitoring	Recommendation
Receipt of food.	Contamination.	Buy from a reputable supplier.	Check goods on receipt.	Check your supplier. Visit their premises if possible, check they are an approved establishment for wholesaling fish (the local EHO will know).
		Packaging intact and clean.	Inspect packaging for damage.	
	Growth of food poisoning organisms.	Delivery temperature of 8°C or colder.	Regularly check air temperature of refrigerator.	Keep records of temperature checks. A temperature of 0-4°C is recommended for wet fish.
Storage.	Contamination.	Keep storage areas clean and in good repair.	Check storage areas and equipment are clean before use and in good repair. Visual checks for contamination.	Use a written cleaning schedule and check list for premises and equipment. See Appendix C for an example.
	Growth of food poisoning organisms.	Keep fish chilled.	Regularly check air temperature of refrigerator.	Keep records of temperature checks.
	Infestation by pests.	Deny access to pests. Control/eradicate existing infestations.	Check regularly for evidence of infestation.	A pest control contractor may be consulted for advice on prevention and proofing.

Step	Hazard	Control Measure	Monitoring	Recommendation
Serving.	Contamination.	Use clean equipment, slicing machine, tongs, trays, scales etc.	Inspect equipment before use.	Use a written cleaning schedule and check list for premises and equipment.
	Growth of food poisoning organisms.	Good personal hygiene, clean hands, clean protective clothing, etc.	Check staff and protective clothing are clean. Check that wash hand basin/bowl has hot water, soap and drying facilities or that there is an adequate supply of sanitised hand-wipes (for mobile/temporary premises).	
Display for sale.	Contamination.	Use clean trays and display units. Protect from contamination from public.	Inspect equipment before use.	Provide screening between food on display and the public.
	Growth of food poisoning organisms.	Display fish at a temperature as close to 0°C as possible.	Regularly check air temperature of refrigerator or check icing arrangements where used.	Keep records of temperature checks carried out.

GREENGROCER

Selling whole fruit and vegetables.

If engaged in further preparation of fruit or vegetables (e.g. ready to cook vegetables or ready to eat fruit/vegetables/salads, etc.), you will need to apply higher food safety and hygiene standards and should consult the checklist for a caterer .

The 'Guide to Compliance' information must be given due consideration by enforcing officers of food authorities when they assess compliance with the Regulations, whereas 'Advice on Good Practice' is simply a recommendation.

The reference column refers to the appropriate page of the Industry Guide to Good Hygiene Practice for Markets and Fairs and to the legislation in the Food Safety (General Food Hygiene) Regulations 1995 and the Food Safety (Temperature Control) Regulations 1995.

Reference should be made to the Glossary of the Industry Guide to Good Hygiene Practice for Markets and Fairs for definitions of terms used in this checklist.

Following the steps below will help to ensure the food you sell from your stall, vehicle or handcart is safe.

Legal requirement	Guide to compliance	Advice on good practice
1. Looking at What You Do	**You must:**	
The Food Safety (General Food Hygiene) Regulations 1995 regulation 4(1)	Carry on your business in a hygienic manner.	
Part 2 regulation 4(3) pages 4-6	Identify the possible problems or hazards that could occur with food in your care (food hazards). Ensure these hazards are controlled and that checks are carried out to ensure the controls are effective.	It is good practice to keep written records of the identified problems, control measures and checks carried out. Examples of possible hazards, their control measures and checks needed for a typical business are given in the table at the end of this checklist.
2. Staff	**You must:**	
Part 3 Chapter X, page 46	Ensure all staff handling food (food handlers) receive adequate instruction and supervision to ensure they know how to do their job hygienically.	Instructions should be repeated at suitable intervals or explained as necessary, as indicated by the observations of supervision.
Part 3 Chapter VIII, 1, 2 and regulation 5, pages 39-41	Provide <u>all</u> staff with information about the standards of personal hygiene they have to maintain and what to do if they are suffering from any skin complaints or stomach upsets. Waterproof dressings must be available for covering open cuts/abrasions. Ensure all staff wear suitable, clean clothing.	High visibility waterproof plasters are recommended. A suitable apron or coat over normal clothing is advisable. Hair should be kept clean and tied back where possible.

Legal requirement	Guide to compliance	Advice on good practice
3. *Care of Food*	**You must:**	
Part 3 *Chapter III, 2(h), page 28* *Chapter IX,1, 2, 3, pages 42-44*	Ensure all fruit and vegetables are fit to eat and are stored correctly to prevent harmful deterioration or contamination. Ensure that if you suspect a batch of food is sub-standard and even after sorting the majority will be unfit, do not bring it onto the premises. If this is discovered on the premises you must set the batch aside, clearly labelled as unfit, store so as not to pose a risk of contamination to any other food, and remove as soon as possible. Ensure all areas are kept clean and tidy and free from pests.	
4. *Premises*	**You must:**	
Part 3 *Chapter I, 2, page 9* *Chapter III, 1, page 20*	Ensure the premises are of adequate size to enable safe and hygienic working conditions.	
Part 3 *Chapter I, 7, page 13* *Chapter III, 1, page 21*	Ensure adequate lighting (natural/ artificial) is provided.	It is recommended that light fittings should be flush mounted, of simple design, corrosion resistant, easily cleaned and designed to prevent broken glass falling onto food.
Part 3 *Chapter I, 5, page 13* *Chapter III, 1, page 21*	Ensure adequate natural or mechanical ventilation is provided.	Reliance upon natural ventilation/market hall ventilation system would be satisfactory in most instances.
Part 3 *Chapter I, 2, page 9* *Chapter III, 1, page 20*	Ensure good layout (in terms of location of storage areas, preparation areas, hand and equipment washing facilities, display area, etc.) to enable the use of good hygiene practices and to make cleaning easy.	
Part 3 *Chapter I, 1, 2, pages 8, 9* *Chapter III, 1, 2(b), (c), (e), pages 20-25* *Chapter V, page 33*	Ensure the premises, food contact surfaces and equipment are kept clean and maintained in good condition. This will involve regular inspection of your premises to identify any structural defects or broken equipment and the arrangement of necessary remedial action. For acceptable surface finishes see Appendix E of the Industry Guide to Good Hygiene Practice for Markets and Fairs, page 133.	Draw up a routine cleaning schedule to ensure that all parts of the premises are thoroughly cleaned on a regular basis.

Legal requirement	Guide to compliance	Advice on good practice
5. Access to Facilities	**You must:**	
Part 3 *Chapter I, 3, 4, pages 11-13* *Chapter III, 2(a) page 22*	Ensure facilities for cleaning hands are available. On permanent stalls, this must be a wash hand basin with hot and cold (or warm) water, soap and a means of drying hands, preferably disposable towels, although the use of communal facilities, where available, is acceptable. Mobile/temporary premises may use bowls. The use of communal facilities with hot and cold running water is acceptable for washing hands and/or any equipment.	On mobile/temporary premises other hand cleaning facilities are acceptable e.g. commercial quality sanitised handwipes.
Chapter II, 2, page 18 *Chapter III, 2(c) page 24*	Where equipment needs to be washed on the premises, to ensure food safety, ensure facilities are provided e.g. sink with hot and cold (or warm) water. On mobile/temporary premises, bowls are acceptable. Equipment and hand-washing facilities may be provided by a single facility provided these activities can be carried out effectively and without prejudice to food safety. The use of communal facilities, where available, is acceptable.	Any equipment used on mobile or temporary premises may be returned to a base depot for cleaning to reduce the number or size of sinks needed.
6. Water Supply	**You must:**	
Part 3 *Chapter III, 2 (e). page 25* *Chapter VII, 1, page 37*	Where washing facilities need to be provided (see above), ensure an adequate supply of potable (drinking) water is provided on the stall/vehicle/handcart, preferably from the mains water supply. Where connection to the mains supply is not possible, water containers may be used. These must be filled from a potable supply. Ensure clean water containers are capable of being cleaned and are cleaned and disinfected regularly.	Clean water containers should be clearly distinguishable from waste water containers.

Legal requirement	Guide to compliance	Advice on good practice
Part 3 *Chapter II, 2, page 18*	Ensure that where hot water is required, there is an adequate potable supply. This can be provided from the main storage system or by an instantaneous gas or electric water heater. Where there are no services to the stall/vehicle/handcart, insulated containers of hot water are acceptable.	
7. Food Contact Surfaces and Equipment (e.g. display areas).	**You must:**	
Part 3 *Chapter II, 1(f) page 17* *Chapter III, 1, 2(b), pages 20-24* *Chapter V, 1, page 33*	Ensure all food contact surfaces and equipment are in good repair, kept clean and have finishes that allow effective cleaning and disinfection. Suitable finishes include stainless steel, ceramics, food grade plastics. Ensure wooden stall counters or proprietary "plastic grass" used for display purposes are maintained in good condition and kept clean. Ensure cardboard, waxed paper or other similar disposable containers used for food transport or display are not re-used where there is a risk of contamination in subsequent use.	
8. Waste Disposal	**You must:**	
Part 3 *Chapter III, 2(f), page 26* *Chapter VI, 1, 2, 3, pages 35-36*	Ensure all waste is stored so that it does not pose a contamination risk to any food or attract insects/pests. Ensure that where there is no possibility of connection to the mains drainage system via a trapped connection, waste water is stored in an enclosed container and disposed of carefully down a suitable foul water drain on site or back at a base depot, so as not to cause a risk of contamination to food.	This will normally involve providing a lidded, washable container.

Other ways of complying with the Regulations may be acceptable - consult your local Environmental Health Officer for advice.

GREENGROCER

FOOD HAZARDS AND THEIR CONTROL

PROCESS Receipt, storage and sale of whole fruit and vegetables.

Note: Supervision, instruction and/or training is applicable at each step.

Step	Hazard	Control Measure	Monitoring	Recommendation
Receipt of food.	Contamination.	Buy from a reputable supplier. Packaging intact and clean.	Check goods on receipt. Inspect packaging for damage.	Check your supplier. Visit their premises if possible.
Storage.	Contamination. Infestation by food pests.	Keep storage areas clean and in good repair. Deny access to pests. Control/eradicate existing infestations.	Check storage areas and equipment are clean before use and in good repair. Visual checks for contamination. Check regularly for evidence of infestation.	Use a written cleaning schedule and checklist for premises and equipment. A pest contractor may be consulted for advice on prevention and proofing.
Serving and display for sale.	Contamination.	Use clean premises and equipment e.g. scoops, bags, display trays. Good personal hygiene e.g. clean hands, clean clothing. Protect from contamination from public.	Check premises and equipment are clean and in good repair. Check staff and clothing are clean. Check that wash hand basin/bowl has hot and cold (or warm) water, soap and drying facilities or that there is an adequate supply of sanitised handwipes (for mobile/ temporary premises).	Use a written cleaning schedule and checklist for premises and equipment. See Appendix C for an example. Draw up a code of personal hygiene standards for staff to follow. Provide screening between food on display and the public.

GROCER CHECKLIST

Selling wrapped or open low risk foods, (e.g. canned or bottled goods, nuts, sweets, cereals or plain bread products).

If high risk foods such as dairy cakes and confectionery are sold you will need to apply higher food safety and hygiene standards and should consult the checklist for a delicatessen.

The 'Guide to Compliance' information must be given due consideration by enforcing officers of food authorities when they assess compliance with the Regulations, whereas 'Advice on Good Practice' is simply a recommendation.

The reference column refers to the appropriate page of the Industry Guide to Good Hygiene Practice for Markets and Fairs and to the legislation in the Food Safety (General Food Hygiene) Regulations 1995 and the Food Safety (Temperature Control) Regulations 1995.

Reference should be made to the Glossary of the Industry Guide to Good Hygiene Practice for Markets and Fairs for definitions of terms used in this checklist.

Following the steps below will help to ensure the food you sell from your stall, vehicle or handcart is safe.

Reference	Guide to compliance	Advice on good practice
1. Looking at What You Do	**You must:**	
The Food Safety (General Food Hygiene) Regulations 1995 regulation 4(1)	Carry on your business in a hygienic manner.	
Part 2 regulation 4(3) pages 4-6	Identify the possible problems or hazards that could occur with food in your care (food hazards). Ensure these hazards are controlled and that checks are carried out to ensure the controls are effective.	It is good practice to keep written records of the identified problems, control measures and checks carried out. Examples of possible hazards, their control measures and checks needed for a typical business are given in the table at the end of this checklist.
2. Staff	**You must:**	
Part 3 Chapter X, page 46	Ensure all staff handling food (food handlers) receive adequate instruction and supervision to ensure they know how to do their job hygienically.	Instructions should be repeated at suitable intervals or explained as necessary, as indicated by the observations of supervision.
Part 3 Chapter VIII 1, 2 and regulation 5, pages 39-41	Provide <u>all</u> staff with information about the standards of personal hygiene they have to maintain and what to do if they are suffering from any skin complaints or stomach upsets. Waterproof dressings must be available for covering open cuts/abrasions. Ensure all staff wear suitable, clean clothing.	High visibility, waterproof plasters are recommended. A suitable apron or coat over normal clothing is advisable. Hair should be kept clean and tied back where possible.

Legal requirement	Guide to compliance	Advice on good practice
3. Care of Food	**You must:**	
Part 3 *Chapter III, 2(h), page 28* *Chapter IX, 1, 2, 3, pages 42-44*	Ensure all food is fit to eat and is stored correctly to prevent harmful deterioration or contamination. Ensure all areas are kept clean and tidy and free from pests.	It is good practice to ensure all food is sold within its 'best before' date.
4. Premises	**You must:**	
Part 3 *Chapter I, 2, page 9* *Chapter III, 1, page 20*	Ensure the premises are of adequate size to enable safe and hygienic working conditions.	
Part 3 *Chapter I, 7, page 13* *Chapter III, 1, page 21*	Ensure adequate lighting (natural/ artificial) is provided.	It is recommended that light fittings should be flush mounted, of simple design, corrosion resistant, easily cleaned and designed to prevent broken glass falling onto food.
Part 3 *Chapter I, 5, page 13.* *Chapter III, 1, page 21*	Ensure adequate natural or mechanical ventilation is provided.	Reliance upon natural ventilation/market hall ventilation system would be satisfactory in most instances.
Part 3 *Chapter I, 2, page 9* *Chapter III, 1, page 20*	Ensure good layout (in terms of location of storage areas, preparation areas, hand and equipment washing facilities, display area, etc.) to enable the use of good hygiene practices and to make cleaning easy.	
Part 3 *Chapter I, 1, 2, pages 8, 9* *Chapter III, 1, 2(b), (c), (e), pages 20-25* *Chapter V, page 33*	Ensure the premises, food contact surfaces and equipment are kept clean and maintained in good condition. This will involve regular inspection of your premises to identify any structural defects or broken equipment and the arrangement of necessary remedial action. For acceptable surface finishes see Appendix E of the Industry Guide to Good Hygiene Practice for Markets and Fairs, page 133.	Draw up a routine cleaning schedule to ensure that all parts of the premises are thoroughly cleaned on a regular basis.

Legal requirement	Guide to compliance	Advice on good practice
5. *Access to Facilities*	**You must:**	
Part 3 *Chapter I, 3, 4, pages 11-13* *Chapter III, 2(a), page 22*	Ensure adequate facilities for cleaning hands are available. On permanent stalls this must be a wash hand basin with hot and cold (or warm) water, soap and a means of drying hands (preferably disposable towels) although the use of communal facilities, where available, is acceptable. Mobile/ temporary premises may use bowls.	On mobile/temporary premises other hand cleaning facilities are acceptable e.g. commercial quality sanitised hand wipes.
Part 3 *Chapter II, 2, page 18* *Chapter III, 2(c), page 24*	Where equipment needs to be washed on the premises to ensure food safety, ensure facilities are provided e.g. sink with hot and cold (or warm) water. On mobile/temporary premises, bowls are acceptable. Equipment and hand washing facilities may be provided by a single facility provided these activities can be carried out effectively and without prejudice to food safety. The use of communal facilities, where available, is acceptable.	Any equipment used on mobile or temporary premises may be returned to a base depot for cleaning to reduce the size or number of sinks needed.
6. *Water Supply*	**You must:**	
Part 3 *Chapter III, 2(e), page 25* *Chapter VII, 1, page 37*	Where washing facilities need to be provided (see above), ensure an adequate supply of potable (drinking) water is provided on the stall/vehicle/handcart, preferably from the mains water supply. Where connection to the mains supply is not possible, water containers may be used. These must be filled from a potable supply. Ensure clean water containers are capable of being cleaned and are cleaned and disinfected regularly.	Clean water containers should be clearly distinguishable from waste water containers.
Part 3 *Chapter II, 2, page 18*	Ensure that where hot water is required, there is an adequate potable supply. This can be provided from the main storage system or by an instantaneous gas or electric water heater. Where there are no services to the stall/vehicle/handcart, insulated containers of hot water are acceptable.	

Legal requirement	Guide to compliance	Advice on good practice
7. Food Contact Surfaces and Equipment *(e.g. display areas, cutting boards, weighing scales, utensils, etc).*	**You must:**	
Part 3 *Chapter II, 1(f), page 17* *Chapter III, 1, 2(b), pages 20-25* *Chapter V, 1, page 33*	Ensure all food contact surfaces and equipment are in good repair, kept clean, and have finishes that allow effective cleaning and disinfection. Suitable finishes include stainless steel, ceramics, food grade plastics. Ensure wooden stall counters used for display purposes are maintained in good condition and kept clean. Ensure cardboard, waxed paper or other similar disposable containers used for food transport or display are not re-used where there is a risk of contamination in subsequent use.	
8. Waste Disposal	**You must:**	
Part 3 *Chapter III, 2(f), page 26* *Chapter VI, 1, 2, 3, pages 35-36*	Ensure all waste is stored so that it does not pose a contamination risk to any food or attract insects/pests. Ensure that where there is no possibility of connection to the mains drainage system via a trapped connection, waste water is stored in an enclosed container and disposed of carefully down a suitable foul water drain on site or back at a base depot so as not to cause a risk of contamination to food.	This will normally involve providing a lidded, washable container.

Other ways of complying with the Regulations may be acceptable - consult your local Environmental Health Officer for advice.

GROCER

FOOD HAZARDS AND THEIR CONTROL

PROCESS Receipt, storage and sale of wrapped, bottled or canned goods and/or open dried goods, plain bread products, fruit and vegetables.

Note: Supervision, instruction and/or training is applicable at each step.

Step	Hazard	Control Measure	Monitoring	Recommendation
Receipt of goods.	Contamination.	Buy from a reputable supplier. Packaging intact and clean.	Check goods on receipt. Inspect packaging for damage.	Check your supplier. Visit their premises if possible. Check 'best before' dates.
Storage.	Contamination. Infestation by food pests. Growth of food poisoning organisms.	Keep storage areas clean and in good repair. Deny access to pests. Control/eradicate existing infestations.	Check storage areas and equipment are clean before use and in good repair. Visual Checks for contamination. Check regularly for evidence of infestation.	Use a written cleaning schedule and check list for premises and equipment. See Appendix C for an example. A pest control contractor may be consulted for advice on prevention and proofing. Check 'best before' dates.
Serving and display.	Contamination.	Premises and equipment clean and in good repair. Good personal hygiene e.g. clean hands, clean clothing. Protect from contamination from public.	Check equipment is clean and in good repair. Check staff and clothing are clean. Check that wash hand basin/bowl has hot and cold (or warm) water, soap and drying facilities or that there is an adequate supply of sanitised handwipes (for mobile/ temporary premises).	Use a written cleaning schedule and check list for premises and equipment. Draw up a code of personal hygiene standards for staff to follow. Provide screening/ wrapping for food on display.

HOT CHESTNUT SELLER CHECKLIST

Selling hot chestnuts only.

If selling any other high risk food you will need to apply higher food safety and hygiene standards and should consult the checklist for a delicatessen

The 'Guide to Compliance' information must be given due consideration by enforcing officers of food authorities when they assess compliance with the Regulations, whereas 'Advice on Good Practice' is simply a recommendation.

The reference column refers to the appropriate page of the Industry Guide to Good Hygiene Practice for Markets and Fairs and to the legislation in the Food Safety (General Food Hygiene) Regulations 1995 and the Food Safety (Temperature Control) Regulations 1995.

Reference should be made to the Glossary of the Industry Guide to Good Hygiene Practice for Markets and Fairs for definitions of terms used in this checklist.

Following the steps below will help to ensure the food you sell from your stall, vehicle or handcart is safe.

Legal requirement	Guide to compliance	Advice on good practice
1. Looking at What You Do	**You must:**	
The Food Safety (General Food Hygiene) Regulations 1995 regulation 4(1)	Carry on your business in a hygienic manner.	
Part 2 regulation 4(3) pages 4-6	Identify the possible problems or hazards that could occur with food in your care (food hazards). Ensure these hazards are controlled and that checks are carried out to ensure the controls are effective.	It is good practice to keep written records of the identified problems, control measures and checks carried out. Examples of possible hazards, their control measures and checks needed for a typical business are given in the table at the end of this checklist.
2. Staff	**You must:**	
Part 3 Chapter X, page 46	Ensure all staff handling food (food handlers) receive adequate instruction and supervision to ensure they know how to do their job hygienically.	Instructions should be repeated at suitable intervals or explained as necessary, as indicated by the observations of supervision.
Part 3 Chapter VIII, 1, 2 and regulation 5, pages 39-41	Provide <u>all</u> staff with information about the standards of personal hygiene they have to maintain and what to do if they are suffering from any skin complaints or stomach upsets. Waterproof dressings must be available for covering open cuts/ abrasions. Ensure all staff wear suitable, clean clothing.	High visibility waterproof plasters are recommended. A suitable apron or coat over normal clothing is advisable. Hair should be kept clean and tied back where possible.

Legal requirement	Guide to compliance	Advice on good practice
3. Care of Food	**You must:**	
Part 3 *Chapter III, 2(h), page 28* *Chapter IX, 1, 2, 3, pages 42-44*	Ensure all chestnuts are fit to eat and are stored correctly to prevent harmful deterioration or contamination. Ensure all areas are kept clean and tidy and free from pests.	There should be no visible signs of damage which could lead to contamination, e.g. split skins leading to mould growth.
4. Premises	**You must:**	
Part 3 *Chapter I, 2, page 9* *Chapter III, 1, page 20*	Ensure the premises are of adequate size to enable safe and hygienic working conditions.	
Part 3 *Chapter I, 7, page 13* *Chapter III, 1, page 21*	Ensure adequate lighting (natural/artificial) is provided.	It is recommended that light fittings should be flush mounted, of simple design, corrosion resistant, easily cleaned and designed to prevent broken glass falling onto food.
Part 3 *Chapter I, 5, page 13* *Chapter III, 1, page 21*	Ensure adequate natural or mechanical ventilation is provided.	Reliance upon natural ventilation/market hall ventilation system is likely to be satisfactory in most instances.
Part 3 *Chapter I, 2, page 9* *Chapter III, 1, page 20*	Ensure good layout (in terms of location of storage areas, preparation areas, hand and equipment washing facilities, display area, etc.) to enable the use of good hygiene practices and to make cleaning easy.	
Part 3 *Chapter I, 1, 2, pages 8, 9* *Chapter III, 1, 2(b), (c), (e), pages 20-25* *Chapter V, page 33*	Ensure the premises food contact surfaces and equipment are kept clean and maintained in good condition. This will involve regular inspection of your premises to identify any structural defects or broken equipment and the arrangement of necessary remedial action. For acceptable surface finishes see Appendix E of the Industry Guide to Good Hygiene Practice for Markets and Fairs, page 133.	Draw up a routine cleaning schedule to ensure that all parts of premises are thoroughly cleaned on a regular basis.

Legal requirement	Guide to compliance	Advice on good practice
5. Access to Facilities	**You must:**	
Part 3 *Chapter I, 3, 4, pages 11-13* *Chapter III, 2(a), page 22*	Ensure facilities for cleaning hands are available. On permanent stalls this must be a wash hand basin with hot and cold (or warm) water, soap and a means of drying hands (preferably disposable towels), although the use of communal facilities, where available, is acceptable. Mobile/temporary premises may use bowls.	On mobile/temporary premises other hand-cleaning facilities are acceptable e.g. commercial quality sanitised handwipes.
Part 3 *Chapter II, 2, page 18* *Chapter III, 2(c) page 24*	Where equipment needs to be washed on the premises to ensure food safety, ensure facilities are provided, e.g. sink with hot and cold (or warm) water. On mobile/temporary premises bowls are acceptable. Equipment and hand washing facilities may be provided by a single facility provided these activities can be carried out effectively and without prejudice to food safety. The use of communal facilities, where available, is acceptable.	Any equipment used on mobile/ temporary premises may be returned to a base depot for cleaning to reduce the size or number of sinks needed.
6. Water Supply	**You must:**	
Part 3 *Chapter III, 2(e), page 25* *Chapter VII, 1, page 37*	Where washing facilities need to be provided (see above), ensure an adequate supply of potable (drinking) water is provided on the stall/vehicle/handcart, preferably from the mains water supply. Where connection to the mains supply is not possible, water containers may be used. These must be filled from a potable supply. Ensure clean water containers are capable of being cleaned and are cleaned and disinfected regularly.	Clean water containers should be clearly distinguishable from waste water containers.
Part 3 *Chapter II, 2, page 18*	Ensure that where hot water is required there is an adequate potable supply. This can be provided from the main storage system or by an instantaneous gas or electric water heater. Where there are no services to the stall/vehicle/handcart, insulated containers of hot water are acceptable.	

Legal requirement	Guide to compliance	Advice on good practice
7. Food Contact Surfaces and Equipment *(e.g. storage containers, cooking equipment, utensils, etc).*	**You must:**	
Part 3 *Chapter II, 1(f), page 17* *Chapter III, 1, 2(b), pages 20-24* *Chapter V, 1, page 33*	Ensure all food contact surfaces and equipment are in good repair, kept clean, and have finishes that allow effective cleaning and disinfection. Suitable finishes include stainless steel, ceramics, food grade plastics. Ensure cardboard, waxed paper or other similar disposable containers used for food transport or display are not re-used where there is a risk of contamination in subsequent use.	
8. Waste Disposal	**You must:**	
Part 3 *Chapter III, 2 (f), page 26* *Chapter VI, 1, 2, 3, pages 35-36*	Ensure all waste is stored so that it does not pose a contamination risk to any food or attract insects/pests. Ensure that where there is no possibility of connection to the mains drainage system via a trapped connection, waste water is stored in an enclosed container and disposed of carefully down a suitable foul water drain, on site or back at a base depot, so as not to cause a risk of contamination to food.	This will normally involve providing a lidded washable container.

Other ways of complying with the Regulations may be acceptable - consult your local Environmental Health Officer for advice.

HOT CHESTNUT SELLER

FOOD HAZARDS AND THEIR CONTROL

PROCESS Receipt, storage, preparation and service of chestnuts.

Note: Supervision, instruction and/or training is applicable at each step.

Step	Hazard	Control Measure	Monitoring	Recommendation
Receipt of food.	Contamination.	Buy from a reputable supplier. Packaging intact and clean.	Check goods on receipt. Inspect packaging for damage.	Check your supplier. Visit their premises if possible.
Storage.	Contamination. Infestation by food pests.	Keep storage areas clean and in good repair. Deny access to pests. Control/eradicate existing infestations.	Check storage areas and equipment are clean before use and in good repair. Visual checks for contamination. Check regularly for evidence of infestation.	Use a written cleaning schedule and check list for premises and equipment. See Appendix C for an example. A pest control contractor may be consulted for advice on prevention and proofing.
Preparation and serving/ display for sale.	Contamination.	Use clean premises and equipment. Good personal hygiene, e.g. clean hands, clean clothing.	Check premises and equipment are in good repair and clean. Check staff and clothing are clean. Check that wash hand basin/bowl has hot and cold (or warm) water, soap and drying facilities or that there is an adequate supply of sanitised handwipes (for mobile/ temporary premises).	Use a written cleaning schedule and check list for premises and equipment. Draw up a code of personal hygiene standards for staff to follow.

ICE CREAM VENDOR CHECKLIST

Selling open ice cream, (i.e. scoop and soft serve ice cream) or wrapped ice cream.

If selling other high risk food you will need to apply higher food safety and hygiene standards and should consult the checklist for a delicatessen.

The 'Guide to Compliance' information must be given due consideration by enforcing officers of food authorities when they assess compliance with the Regulations, whereas 'Advice on Good Practice' is simply a recommendation.

The reference column refers to the appropriate page of the Industry Guide to Good Hygiene Practice for Markets and Fairs and to the legislation in the Food Safety (General Food Hygiene) Regulations 1995 and the Food Safety (Temperature Control) Regulations 1995.

Reference should be made to the Glossary of the Industry Guide to Good Hygiene Practice for Markets and Fairs for definitions of terms used in this checklist.

Following the steps below will help to ensure the food you sell from your stall, vehicle or handcart is safe.

Reference	Guide to compliance	Advice on good practice
1. Looking at What You Do	**You must:**	
The Food Safety (General Food Hygiene) Regulations 1995 regulation 4(1)	Carry on your business in a hygienic manner.	
Part 2 regulation 4(3) pages 4-6	Identify the possible problems or hazards that could occur with food in your care (food hazards). Ensure these hazards are controlled and that checks are carried out to ensure the controls are effective.	It is good practice to keep written records of the identified problems, control measures and checks carried out. Examples of possible hazards, their control measures and checks needed for a typical business are given in the table at the end of this checklist.
2. Staff	**You must:**	
Part 3 Chapter X, page 46	Ensure all staff handling food (food handlers) receive adequate instruction and supervision to ensure they know how to do their job hygienically.	Instructions should be repeated at suitable intervals or explained as necessary as indicated by the observations of supervision.
Part 3 Chapter VIII, 1, 2 and regulation 5, pages 39-41	Provide <u>all</u> staff with information about the standards of personal hygiene they have to maintain and what to do if they are suffering from any skin complaints or stomach upsets. Waterproof dressings must be available for covering open cuts/abrasions. Ensure all staff wear clean, suitable clothing. This will be fulfilled by: ● staff handling open ice-cream - clean, protective overclothing and head covering to contain hair. ● staff handling wrapped ice-cream - clean clothing.	High visibility waterproof plasters are recommended. Protective clothing should preferably cover the arms and body.

Reference	Guide to compliance	Advice on good practice
3. *Care of Food*	**You must:**	
Part 3 *Chapter III, 2(g), (h), page 27, 28* *Chapter IX, 1, 2, 3, pages 42-44* *Ice cream (Heat Treatment etc.) Regulations 1959*	Ensure all ice cream is fit to eat and is stored correctly to prevent harmful deterioration or contamination. Serving ice cream which has gone above a temperature of -2.2°C is illegal - melted ice cream should never be re-frozen. Store fresh pasteurised mixes at 7.2°C or below, until the freezing process begins. Ensure all areas are kept clean and tidy and free from pests. Protect open ice cream, on display, from contamination e.g. by covering or providing a 'sneeze screen'.	If ice cream shows any sign of melting, discard it and report the fact to your supervisor/supplier. It is good practice to ensure all food is used within its 'best before' date. Ideally, ice cream should be kept at or below -18°C in bulk storage and at or below -15°C in scooping cabinets. Fresh pasteurised mixes are best stored at between 1°C and 4°C.
4. *Premises*	**You must:**	
Part 3 *Chapter I, 2, page 9* *Chapter III, 1, page 20*	Ensure the premises are of adequate size to enable safe and hygienic working conditions.	
Part 3 *Chapter I , 7, page 13* *Chapter III, 1, page 21*	Ensure adequate lighting (natural/ artificial) is provided.	It is recommended that light fittings should be flush mounted, of simple design, corrosion resistant, easily cleaned and designed to prevent broken glass falling onto food.
Part 3 *Chapter I, 5, page 13* *Chapter III, 1, page 21*	Ensure adequate natural or mechanical ventilation is provided.	Reliance upon natural ventilation/market hall ventilation system is likely to be satisfactory in most instances.
Part 3 *Chapter I, 2, page 9* *Chapter III, 1, page 20*	Ensure good layout (in terms of location of storage areas, preparation areas, hand and equipment washing facilities, display area, etc.) to enable the use of good hygiene practices and to make cleaning easy.	

Reference	Guide to compliance	Advice on good practice
Part 3 *Chapter I, 1, 2, pages 8, 9* *Chapter III, 1, 2(b), (c), (e),* *pages 20-25* *Chapter V, page 33*	Ensure the premises food contact surfaces and equipment are kept clean and maintained in good condition. Food contact surfaces must be capable of being disinfected. This will involve regular inspection of your premises to identify any structural defects or broken equipment and the arrangement of necessary remedial action. For acceptable surface finishes see Appendix E of the Industry Guide to Good Hygiene Practice for Markets and Fairs, page 133.	Draw up a routine cleaning schedule to ensure that all parts of the premises are thoroughly cleaned on a regular basis. The driver's cab in a mobile vehicle should be kept clean and should be separated from the rest of the vehicle where possible.
5. Access to Facilities	**You must:**	
Part 3 *Chapter I, 3, 4, pages 11-13* *Chapter III, 2(a), page 22*	When open ice cream is sold, ensure facilities for cleaning hands are provided on the stall/vehicle/handcart. This must be a wash hand basin with hot and cold (or warm) water, soap and a means of drying hands (preferably disposable towels). Mobile/temporary premises may use bowls. When selling only wrapped ice cream, the use of communal facilities, where available, is acceptable.	Temporary/mobile premises selling only wrapped ice cream may use other hand-cleaning facilities e.g. sanitised wipes.
Part 3 *Chapter II, 2, page 18* *Chapter III, 2(c), page 24*	Where equipment needs to be washed on the premises to ensure food safety, ensure facilities are provided e.g. sink with hot and cold (or warm) water. On mobile/temporary premises bowls are acceptable. When only wrapped ice cream is sold, communal facilities may be used, where available. The equipment and hand washing facilities must be separate when open ice-cream is handled.	Any equipment used on mobile/temporary premises may be returned to a base depot for cleaning to reduce the size or number of sinks needed.
6. Water Supply	**You must:**	
Part 3 *Chapter III, 2(e), page 25* *Chapter VII, 1, page 37*	Where washing facilities need to be provided (see above), ensure an adequate supply of potable (drinking) water is provided on the stall/vehicle/ handcart, preferably from the mains water supply. Where connection to the mains supply is not possible, water containers may be used. These must be filled from a potable supply. Ensure clean water containers are capable of being cleaned and are cleaned and disinfected regularly.	Clean water containers should be clearly distinguishable from waste water containers.

Reference	Guide to compliance	Advice on good practice
Part 3 *Chapter II, 2, page 18* *Chapter I, 4, page 12*	Ensure that where hot water is required there is an adequate supply. This can be provided from the main storage system or by an instantaneous gas or electric water heater. Where there are no services to the stall/vehicle/handcart, insulated containers of hot water are acceptable. It is recommended that hot and cold water are piped to the washing facilities.	
7. Food Contact Surfaces and Equipment (e.g. display areas, freezers, ice cream containers, utensils).	**You must:**	
Part 3 *Chapter II, 1(f), page 17* *Chapter III, 1, 2(b), pages 20-24* *Chapter V, 1, page 33*	Ensure all food contact surfaces and equipment are in good repair, kept clean and have finishes that allow effective cleaning and disinfection. Suitable finishes include stainless steel, ceramics, food grade plastics. Ensure cardboard, waxed paper or other similar disposable containers used for food transport or display are not re-used where there is a risk of contamination in subsequent use.	Containers should be used for storing scoops and for rinsing scoops after serving. Both should contain sanitising solutions which are approved for food use and should be emptied and refilled at least once an hour. Do not use chlorine based sanitisers with aluminium utensils. The cleaning of soft-serve ice cream freezers should be carried out according to manufacturers instructions.
8. Waste Disposal	**You must:**	
Part 3 *Chapter III, 2 (f), page 26* *Chapter VI, 1, 2, 3, pages 35-36*	Ensure all waste is stored so that it does not pose a contamination risk to any food or attract insects/pests. Ensure that where there is no possibility of connection to the mains drainage system via a trapped connection, waste water is stored in an enclosed container and disposed of carefully down a suitable foul water drain on site or back at a base depot so as not to cause a risk of contamination to food.	This will normally involve providing a lidded, washable container.

More detailed advice and information can be found in 'A Guide to the Safe Handling and Service of Ice Cream' produced by the Ice Cream Alliance, see Reference section of the Industry Guide to Good Hygiene Practice for Markets and Fairs.

Other ways of complying with the Regulations may be acceptable - consult your local Environmental Health Officer for advice.

ICE CREAM VENDOR

FOOD HAZARDS AND THEIR CONTROL

PROCESS Receipt, storage, preparation and service of ice cream.

Note: Supervision, instruction and/or training is applicable at each step.

Step	Hazard	Control Measure	Monitoring	Recommendation
Receipt of food.	Contamination.	Buy from a reputable supplier.	Check goods on receipt.	Check your supplier. Visit their premises if possible.
		Packaging intact and clean.	Inspect packaging for damage.	Check 'best before' dates.
	Growth of food poisoning organisms.	Reject products not at a delivery temperature of -2.2°C or below for frozen ice cream, 7.2°C or below for a pasteurised mix.	Check delivery temperature, the air temperature of the vehicle or 'between pack' temperature of products.	Keep records of temperature checks.
Storage.	Contamination.	Premises and equipment clean and in good repair.	Check storage areas and equipment are clean before use and in good repair.	Use a written cleaning schedule and check list for premises and equipment. See Appendix C for an example.
	Growth of food poisoning organisms.	Keep frozen ice cream and pasteurised mixes at -2.2°C or below and 7.2°C or below respectively.	Check air temperature of fridges/freezers throughout the day. Check 'best before' dates daily.	Check and keep records of daily temperature of chilled storage units. Ideally, ice cream should be kept at or below -18°C in bulk storage and at or below -15°C in scooping cabinets.
	Infestation by food pests.	Deny access to pests. Control/eradicate existing infestations.	Check regularly for evidence of infestation.	A pest control contractor may be consulted for advice on prevention and proofing.

Step	Hazard	Control Measure	Monitoring	Recommendation
Preparation.	Growth of food poisoning bacteria.	Limit preparation times and time the product is out of the fridge/ freezer.	Check food handling practices and preparation times regularly.	
	Contamination.	Good personal hygiene of all food handlers e.g. clean hands, clean protective clothing.	Check staff and protective clothing are clean. Check that wash hand basin has hot and cold (or warm) water, soap and drying facilities or that there is an adequate supply of sanitised handwipes (for mobile/ temporary premises).	Draw up a code of personal hygiene standards for staff to follow.
		Premises and equipment kept clean and in good repair.	Inspect premises and equipment to ensure they are clean and in good repair. Visual checks for contamination.	Use a written cleaning schedule and checklist for premises and equipment.
Serving/ display for sale.	Contamination.	Use clean equipment, containers, display units etc.	Check equipment is in good repair and clean.	Use a written cleaning schedule and check list for premises and equipment.
	Growth of food poisoning organisms.	Good personal hygiene, clean hands, protective clothing, etc.	Check staff and protective clothing are clean. Check that wash hand basin/bowl has hot and cold (warm) water, soap and drying facilities or that there is an adequate supply of sanitised handwipes (for mobile/ temporary premises).	Draw up a code of personal hygiene standards for staff to follow.
		Display for sale at -2.2°C or colder.	Regularly check fridge/food temperature.	Keep records of temperature checks.
		Protect from contamination from public.	Check screening/ wrapping of food on display.	

Introduction

For the purposes of the Regulations and Temperature Regulations, a food business means any undertaking, whether carried on for profit or not and whether public or private, carrying out any or all of the following operations, namely, preparation, processing, manufacture, packaging, storage, transportation, distribution, handling or offering for sale or supply of food.

As such, operators of markets and fairs do not necessarily fall within the definition of a food business. However, the Food Safety Act 1990, section 20 contains the provision that if an offence under these Regulations is due to the act or default of some person other than the proprietor of the food business, then the enforcement authority can take legal proceedings against that person.

If under the terms of any lease, licence or agreement a market or fair operator provides facilities (e.g. waste disposal, w.c's, washing facilities) for use by food businesses then those facilities must comply with these Regulations. Unless otherwise stated, it will be the responsibility of the market or fair operator to ensure that the facilities comply with the Regulations and Temperature Regulations.

This section aims to give good practice advice on the range of facilities and services normally provided by operators of markets and fairs for use by food businesses.

1. CLEANING

Those areas for which the operator is responsible must be kept sufficiently clean, so as not to pose a potential threat of contamination of food:

e.g.
- market hall ceilings/girder work/changing rooms;
- compactors/refuse bays;
- loading bays/storage areas;
- goods lifts;
- public areas.

"Food Safe" cleaning chemicals should be used on any surfaces which come into direct contact with food.

2. COMMUNAL FACILITIES

Where communal facilities are provided for food businesses the market/fair operator must ensure that those facilities are maintained to the standard required by the Regulations and Temperature Regulations:

e.g.
- traders toilets'/rest rooms/hand washing facilities/changing rooms;
- cold stores;
- boning out/preparation areas;
- ice making facilities;
- vehicle washing areas;
- equipment washing areas.

Separate facilities for hand, equipment and food washing should be provided and designated according to use. Consideration should also be given to the ratio of stalls/traders and number of these facilities provided. Some guidance is available from the Workplace (Health, Safety and Welfare) Regulations 1992. It should be clear as to whether it is the market/fair operators' or traders' responsibility to provide soap and hand drying facilities.

Detailed cleaning and, where necessary, disinfecting schedules should be drawn up. These should identify the standard and frequency of cleaning and those responsible for carrying out and monitoring of the cleaning.

3. HAZARD ANALYSIS

It may be appropriate for market/fair operators to carry out hazard analysis of their facilities, in line with regulation 4(3) of the Regulations, in relation to any hazards that might impact on food businesses trading from their premises.

4. MANAGING TRADERS

The reputation and hence viability of a market/fair is affected by the conduct of all the traders operating in it. Market/fair operators have a key role to play in ensuring that public confidence in the quality of goods and services provided by this sector is maintained and enhanced:

e.g.
- a working relationship should be developed with enforcement officers in terms of complaints procedures, routine inspections, input into development work, training, etc;
- a clear separation of duties and responsibilities should be drawn up between market/fair operators and traders;
- food traders should be made aware of the Regulations, Temperature Regulations and this Guide, and the requirement to comply with the provisions built into their agreement. Where there is persistent breach of these Regulations, market/fair operators may look to revoking traders' licences/agreements.

5. PEST CONTROL

It is vital that adequate and safe pest control procedures are in place. Professional advice should be sought where necessary to ensure that those areas for which market/fair operators are responsible are adequately protected:

e.g.
- access to birds/insects through windows/ventilation grilles to market halls;
- rodent activity around refuse areas;
- pigeons and other birds around refuse areas;
- rat activity in drains and sewers;
- insect infestations associated with birds nesting/roosting in buildings;
- feral cat populations;
- vacant areas of premises which, if inadequately maintained, may permit pest infestation.

6. REPAIRS AND MAINTENANCE

Market/fair operators should ensure that all repair and maintenance work for which they are responsible, associated with food businesses, is carried out quickly and to the standard required by the Regulations and Temperature Regulations.

Programmed inspection of premises is recommended to ensure that buildings, stalls and facilities are maintained to the appropriate standards.

7. SECURITY

Market/fair operators should ensure that there is adequate security provision to protect foodstuffs from the risk of contamination, (e.g. during loading/unloading of vehicles, and around warehouses/storage areas).

8.   VENTILATION/AIR CONDITIONING

In some cases it may be more appropriate for adequate ventilation/heating/air conditioning to be provided to a market hall rather than to individual food businesses. If this is the case, then the responsibilities for the provision and maintenance must be clearly established between the market/fair operator and the traders:

e.g.
- heat loss/gain through windows and glass roofs;
- heat emission from cooking/refrigeration equipment;
- heat loss through service access points.

9.   WASTE DISPOSAL

Market/fair operators should ensure that adequate waste disposal facilities are available for solid and liquid waste disposal at all sites.

In assessing adequacy they will need to consider:

- risk of cross contamination;
- pest control;
- recycling requirements;
- "Duty of Care" provisions of the Environmental Protection Act 1990;
- public safety;
- quantities of refuse and frequency of collections;
- packaging waste regulations.

Central refuse stores provided by operators of markets or fairs should be:

- kept clean and tidy with daily washing of the openings to chutes and floor areas around chutes, skips, bins, etc.

- managed and supervised. The area for communal use should be supervised to ensure it is kept clean and not misused.

- kept free from pests such as rats, mice and birds. Bins should be lidded, compactor areas should be physically separate from where food is stored, prepared or sold. Any accommodation should be proofed against access by pests. Regular cleaning should reduce problems of flies and insects.

- the area around refuse stores should be capable of being swilled down, kept clear of weeds and well lit.

- external refuse stores should be on a hardstanding.

- liquid waste contained in holding tanks must be discharged carefully so that there is no risk of food contamination.

- grease and oil should not be disposed of down a drain but should be dealt with by a specialist contractor.

10. WATER SUPPLY/DRAINAGE

For the purposes of the Regulations there must be a continuous supply of potable water (drinking) to ensure foodstuffs are not contaminated,

e.g. for:
- washing of food/equipment;
- ice making;
- personal hygiene;
- steam production;
- cleaning;
- cooking.

Where possible food businesses should be provided with water that comes directly from the mains supply.

If a mains supply is not available then food businesses can use containers of water which can be filled from the mains supply, water tanks/bowsers, or a private water supply.

Where the market or fair operator provides water tanks/bowsers they must ensure that they are regularly cleaned and disinfected and filled from a potable supply.

If access to a private water supply is provided they must check with the land owner or food authority that the water is potable.

Where water which is *unfit for drinking* is used (e.g. for the generation of steam, refrigeration, fire control) it must be conducted in separate systems, readily identifiable and having no connection with, nor any possibility of, reflux into the potable water systems.

Where provided ice machines must be regularly cleaned as should containers and utensils used to store and dispense ice.

FOOD HAZARDS AND THEIR CONTROL CHECKLIST

HAZARD ANALYSIS

NAME OF PERSON CARRYING OUT ANALYSIS ....

NAME AND ADDRESS OF BUSINESS ....

TYPE OF FOOD BUSINESS/PROCESS ....

SIGNATURE .... Date ....

Step	Hazard	Control Measure	Monitoring	Recommendation

TEMPERATURE CONTROL RECORD SHEET

DAY	TIME	FRIDGE 1	FRIDGE 2	FREEZER 1	FREEZER 2	DISPLAY CABINET	PERSON RESPONSIBLE	CHECKED BY
Sun	1							
Date	2							
	3							
Mon	1							
Date	2							
	3							
Tue	1							
Date	2							
	3							
Wed	1							
Date	2							
	3							
Thur	1							
Date	2							
	3							
Fri	1							
Date	2							
	3							
Sat	1							
Date	2							
	3							

APPENDIX C

SAMPLE CLEANING SCHEDULE

Equipment/ Area	Cleaning Product	Routine	Frequency	H&S Precautions (Refer to product label)	Person Responsible (Nominate)	Checked By (Nominate)
Floor		All spillages should be dealt with immediately. At the end of each day sweep and wash with hot water and detergent.	Daily			
Walls - behind work surfaces		Clean as you go during the day. Before preparing ready to eat food and at the end of each day, wash with hot water and detergent, rinse with clean hot water and apply sanitiser*.	Daily			
- high and low level		Wash with hot water and detergent.	Weekly			
Ceiling		Wash with hot water and detergent.	Periodically**			
Doors		Wash with hot water and detergent.	Periodically**			
Windows		Wash with hot water and detergent.	Periodically**			
Work Surfaces		Clean as you go during the day. Before preparing ready to eat food and at the end of each day, wash all surfaces with hot water and detergent, rinse with clean hot water, and apply sanitiser.*	Daily			
Sinks		Clean as you go during the day. At the end of each day scour, wash with hot water and detergent, and rinse. Where sinks are used for food, equipment and hand washing, they must be cleaned and disinfected* between uses.	Daily			
Refrigerator		Spillages should be dealt with immediately. Scrub the shelves and wash the food compartments with hot water and detergent, rinse with clean hot water and apply sanitiser.* Defrost according to manufacturers instructions.	Weekly			

　Food Safety (General Food Hygiene) Regulations 1995 – Guide to compliance for Markets & Fairs

Equipment/Area	Cleaning Product	Routine	Frequency	H&S Precautions (Refer to product label)	Person Responsible (Nominate)	Checked By (Nominate)
Storage/Display Shelves		Spillages should be dealt with immediately. Wash with hot water and detergent. If used for both cooked and uncooked food, wash with hot water and detergent, rinse and apply sanitiser.*	Weekly (wrapped, tinned, bottled goods). Daily (unwrapped food, wrapped high risk food).			
Oven		Clean all internal surfaces with proprietary cleaner.	Weekly			
Microwave Oven		Wash all internal surfaces with hot water and detergent, including door, door seals and turntable.	Daily			
Freezer		Wash all internal surfaces with hot water and detergent and rinse with clean hot water. Defrost according to manufacturers instructions.	Periodically**			
Waste Containers		Scrub with hot water and detergent.	Weekly			
External Surfaces		Scrub with hot water and detergent.	Weekly			
Wiping Cloths		Preferably use disposable cloths. If not, change cloths frequently. Boil/soak in sterilising solution at end of each day.	Daily			

* 'Sanitiser' is a disinfectant which is suitable for use on food contact surfaces, i.e. it is non-toxic and non-tainting. Combined detergent/sanitisers may be used in a single stage process.

** 'Periodically' means 'as necessary' and should relate to the build up of dirt.

PRE-EMPLOYMENT MEDICAL QUESTIONNAIRE

1.	Have you now, or have you over the last seven days, suffered from diarrhoea and/or vomiting?	YES/NO
2.	At present, are you suffering from:	
i)	skin trouble affecting hands, arms or face?	YES/NO
ii)	boils, styes or septic fingers?	YES/NO
iii)	discharge from eye, ear or gums/mouth?	YES/NO
3.	Do you suffer from:	
i)	recurring skin or ear trouble?	YES/NO
ii)	a recurring bowel disorder?	YES/NO
4.	Have you ever had, or are you now known to be a carrier of, typhoid or paratyphoid?	YES/NO
5.	In the last 21 days have you been in contact with anyone, at home or abroad, who may have been suffering from typhoid or paratyphoid?	YES/NO

NOTE   If any of the answers to the above questions is given as "Yes", this individual should not be employed as a food handler until medical advice has been obtained.

SOURCE: Food Handlers: Fitness To Work,
Department of Health Guidance Document

APPENDIX E

Examples of Acceptable Surface Finishes

Guidance has been divided into acceptable surfaces for general food premises rooms, (e.g. warehouses, storerooms) in Table A; those for food preparation rooms in Table B and those in mobile and temporary premises in Table C.

These are examples only and alternative surface finishes may be acceptable.

TABLE A

Food storage areas (e.g. warehouses and back up stores/storage rooms) in permanent food premises (not temporary stalls, outdoor stalls and mobile vehicles).

Type of Food Stored	Floors	Walls	Ceilings	Shelves
Pre-wrapped or pre-packaged, tinned, bottled or canned goods only.	Wooden floors or concrete in good condition i.e. smooth level surface, preferably sealed with washable, non toxic product; polymer cement.	Good quality brick or block work free of ledges and gaps, with mortar in good condition preferably sealed with washable paint.	Painted inner surface of roof structure. Painted plaster. Direct fixed or suspended ceiling systems for food premises.	Wood or metal, preferably sealed by paint or varnish, or rustproof.
Open low risk food (e.g. whole fruit and vegetables, dried nuts, sweets etc.) which is not completely covered and contamination is possible.	Sealed concrete, granolithic, terrazzo or quarry tiles. Sealed (painted or varnished) wooden washable floor.	Smooth, block or brickwork or plaster, sealed with waterproof paint.	Waterproof painted plaster, direct fixed or suspended ceiling system capable of periodic cleaning.	Sealed wood or rustproof metal.
Open high risk food which is not completely covered to eliminate contamination.	Well sealed concrete, granolithic or terrazzo tiles, epoxy resin. Where there is no frequent wetting, heavy duty wearing ceramic or vinyl tiles or vinyl sheeting may be used.	Waterproof painted smooth plaster, epoxy resin wall coating, plastic cladding, fibreglass, stainless steel, ceramic tiles (if not prone to impact damage).	Waterproof painted plaster, direct fixed or suspended ceiling system capable of periodic cleaning.	Sealed wood or rust proof metal or proprietary plastic coated shelving or worktop (e.g. melamine).

APPENDIX E

TABLE B

Food preparation areas - including retail display where weighing/cutting and wrapping of food is carried out and cooking and cooling (excluding mobile and temporary premises and outdoor temporary stalls).

Type of Food	Floors	Walls	Ceilings	Food Contact Surfaces
Fruit and vegetables, grocery, bread and confectionery, and dried goods. (No open high risk food).	Flooring tiles (quarry, ceramic or vinyl), vinyl safety flooring, terrazzo, granolithic, cast in situ epoxy resin flooring.	Waterproof painted plaster, ceramic tiles, stainless steel or PVC or similar sheeting. Epoxy resin or similar coating.	Waterproof painted plaster, direct fixed or suspended proprietary ceiling systems designed for food handling areas. In grocery and fruit and vegetable stalls painted inner surface of roof acceptable.	*Display Surfaces* Painted wood and plastics. Plastic grass acceptable in fruit and vegetable stores. *Preparation Surfaces* Hard wearing proprietary work surfaces (e.g. melamine).
Raw fish and meat.	Granolithic, quarry or terrazzo tiles, well sealed concrete (with concrete hardener or epoxy resin floor paint) epoxy resin (particularly good in frequently wet areas). Care must be taken when floors are frequently wet to choose floor surfaces which are not slippery when wet. Vinyl tiles or sheeting may be used but may be damaged if the floor is frequently wet.	Smooth waterproof painted plaster, epoxy resin coating, PVC or similar cladding or stainless steel sheets, ceramic tiles. Immediately behind work surfaces should not be painted plaster but one of the other options.	Waterproof painted plaster, direct fixed or suspended proprietary ceiling capable of being cleaned.	Stainless steel, durable plastic coated shelving or work surfaces (e.g. melamine).
Open high risk food (e.g. caterers, delicatessens, snack and sandwich bars, and others selling ready to eat high risk foods).	Flooring tiles (quarry, ceramic or vinyl), vinyl safety flooring, terrazzo, cast in situ resin flooring, vinyl tiles (but not adjacent to hot equipment).	Washable painted plaster, epoxy resin and similar coating, ceramic tiles, stainless steel sheeting, PVC and similar plastic type sheeting.	Washable painted plaster, direct fixed or suspended ceiling system designed for food handling area.	Stainless steel, durable plastic coated shelves and worktops (e.g. melamine).

APPENDIX E

TABLE C

Mobiles, tents, handcarts and temporary stalls.

The floors' column relates to the floor of a mobile premises or vehicle or a temporary floor to be provided under and/or adjacent to stalls/handcarts and in tents or marquees, for the purposes of ensuring food safety. All floor surfaces should be non-slip (also when wet, if frequently wet).

The walls' column refers to the internal vertical surfaces of mobiles, vehicles, tents, marquees and the upright framework and any vertical screens provided to the sides of stalls/handcarts for the purposes of preventing contamination of food.

The ceilings' column refers to the internal surface of the roof of mobiles, vehicles, marquees and tents, and any framework and cover provided over stalls or handcarts, for the purposes of ensuring food safety.

Type of Food	Floors	Walls/ Vertical Framework	Ceilings/ Cover	Food Contact Surfaces
Pre-wrapped tinned, bottled, packaged goods.	*Outdoor Stalls and Handcarts* Wooden or synthetic duckboards or concrete flags/ tarmac.	*Outdoor Stalls and Handcarts* Wood in good condition, preferably painted or varnished (no splintering). Rust proof metal or perspex-type materials. Full screening not necessary (framework only).	*Outdoor Stalls and Handcarts* Canvas or heavy duty polythene cover or large umbrella. (Not necessary for food safety but may be for health and safety).	*Outdoor Stalls and Handcarts* Wooden, metal or plastic surfaces. Surfaces on which wrapped food is placed must not pose a physical contamination risk (e.g. good condition, free from potential wood/metal/rust splinters).
	Mobile Vehicles Wooden, metal, vinyl covered (splinter and rust free).	*Mobile Vehicles* Metal, wood clad or vinyl clad (splinter and rust free).	*Mobile Vehicles* Metal or wood or vinyl clad.	*Mobile Vehicles* Wooden, metal or plastic surfaces. Surfaces on which wrapped food is placed must not pose a physical contamination risk (e.g. good condition, free from potential wood/metal/rust splinters).
	Tents/marquees Wooden or synthetic duckboards or concrete flags around food display/serving areas.	*Tents/marquees* Tent fabric or canvas (good condition and kept clean).	*Tents/marquees* Tent fabric or canvas (good condition) and kept clean.	*Tents/marquees* Wooden, metal or plastic surfaces. Surfaces on which wrapped food is placed must not pose a physical contamination risk (e.g. good condition, free from potential wood/metal/rust splinters).

Type of Food	Floors	Walls/ Vertical Framework	Ceilings/ Cover	Food Contact Surfaces
Open low risk food.	*Outdoor Stalls and Handcarts* Wooden or synthetic duckboards or concrete flags/ tarmac.	*Outdoor Stalls and Handcarts* Waterproof painted or varnished wood or washable rust proof metal, heavy plastic sheeting, perspex-type material. Adequate screening must ensure food is protected from contamination.	*Outdoor Stalls and Handcarts* Waterproof canvas, polythene cover or umbrella. Adequate screen/material must ensure food is protected from contamination - durable plastic material.	*Outdoor Stalls and Handcarts* *Display:* Waterproof wood, metal or plastic fabric. *Preparation:* Durable plastic or stainless steel surface.
	Mobile Vehicles Wooden or metal (preferably sealed to be waterproof) or vinyl covered.	*Mobile Vehicles* Waterproof painted or varnished wood, washable vinyl or metal. Adequate screening must ensure food is protected from contamination.	*Mobile Vehicles* Waterproof painted or varnished wood or washable vinyl. Adequate screening of food must ensure protection from contamination (e.g. flyscreens to sky-lights).	*Mobile Vehicles* *Display:* Waterproof wood, metal or plastic material. *Preparation:* Durable plastic or stainless steel surface.
	Tents/Marquees Wooden or synthetic duckboards or concrete flags around food display/serving areas.	*Tents/Marquees* Tent fabric or canvas (in good condition and kept clean). This should be treated, if necessary, to ensure it is non-absorbent and easily cleaned up to a height where it could come into contact with food.	*Tents/Marquees* Tent fabric or canvas (good condition and kept clean).	*Tents/Marquees* *Display:* Waterproof wood, metal or plastic material. *Preparation:* Durable plastic or stainless steel surface.
Open high risk food.	*Outdoor Stalls and Handcarts* Sealed wooden or synthetic duckboards with waterproof sheeting underneath, or vinyl or linoleum sheet.	*Outdoor Stalls and Handcarts* Waterproof painted or varnished wood, washable rustproof metal, heavy plastic sheeting or perspex-type. Adequate screening of food must ensure protection from contamination.	*Outdoor Stalls and Handcarts* Waterproof canvas, heavy duty plastic/polythene cover or umbrella.	*Outdoor Stalls and Handcarts* *Display:* Waterproof wood or metal, plastic material. *Preparation:* Durable plastic, ceramic or stainless steel surface.

Type of Food	Floors	Walls/ Vertical Framework	Ceilings/ Cover	Food Contact Surfaces
	Mobile Vehicles Vinyl sheet or tiles preferable. Well sealed waterproof wooden floor acceptable (if not frequently wet) but is not ideal due to wear.	*Mobile Vehicles* Waterproof painted or varnished wood, stainless steel sheeting, plastic cladding or vinyl lining (wall surfaces behind preparation areas should be protected with stainless steel or durable smooth plastic cladding).	*Mobile Vehicles* Waterproof sealed wood or metal or vinyl lining.	*Mobile Vehicles* *Display:* Stainless steel or, where cold food only, plastic or waterproof painted wood. *Preparation:* Durable plastic, ceramic or stainless steel.
	Tents/Marquees Sealed wooden or synthetic duckboard with waterproof sheeting underneath, or vinyl/linoleum type washable sheeting.	*Tents/Marquees* Walls adjacent to preparation areas should be sealed or lined to be waterproof and easily cleaned, up to a height where it may come into contact with food. Tent fabric or canvas (in good condition and kept clean).	*Tents/Marquees* Tent fabric or canvas (good condition and kept clean).	*Tents/Marquees* *Display:* Stainless steel or where cold food only, plastic, waterproof painted wood. *Preparation:* Durable plastic, ceramic or stainless steel.

GLOSSARY

Glossary	Definition
Bacteria	A group of single cell living organisms. Some may spoil food and some may actually cause illness.
Bactericidal detergent	A bactericide is a 'bacteria killer', the same, in practice as a disinfectant. Bactericidal detergents can be used for hand or equipment washing. They remove dirt and destroy micro-organisms. Their effectiveness is often reduced by heavy soiling and it is therefore preferable to clean then disinfect as a two stage process.
Best before date	Date mark required on longer life foods that are not subject to microbiological spoilage (e.g. canned or frozen foods). This date mark relates to quality rather than safety.
Bowser	Closed tank on wheels used to carry water.
Carrier	A person who has been ill with food poisoning and now shows no sign of illness, but may still be carrying food poisoning bacteria in their gut. They are capable of transmitting this bacteria to other people.
Cleaning schedule	A written document outlining how a food premises is to be kept clean. It will include details of each area or piece of equipment to be cleaned, the cleaning product to be used, the person responsible for carrying out the cleaning, the standard of cleanliness required, the frequency of cleaning and any Health and Safety precautions to be taken when handling the cleaning products. Everyone concerned should be made aware of their individual responsibilities and a responsible person should check that the cleaning schedule is followed.
Communal facilities	Facilities provided by the market/fair operator, intended to be used by the traders, often as an alternative to each trader providing their own facilities. Examples include toilets, washing facilities, cold stores, vehicle washing areas, ice-making facilities and central refuse stores.
Condensation	The formation of water droplets as a result of the contact between warm moist air such as steam and a comparatively cooler surface.
Contamination	The introduction or occurrence in food of any microbial pathogens, chemicals, foreign material, spoilage agents, taints, unwanted or diseased matter which may compromise its safety or wholesomeness.
Coving	Rounded finish to the junctions between walls and floors or between two walls. The aim is to make cleaning easier.
Control measures	The actions to be taken to remove an identified hazard or reduce it to a safe level.
Critical points	Steps at which hazards must be controlled to ensure that they are eliminated or reduced to a safe level.
Critical control point	This is the step in the preparation of the food which has to be carried out correctly to ensure that a hazard is removed or reduced to a safe level.
Cross contamination	The transfer of germs from contaminated (usually raw) foods to other foods. This may be: ● by direct contact. (They are stored next to each other); ● by drip. (One is stored above the other); ● by food handlers. (Who handle one then the other); ● by equipment and work surfaces. (Used first for contaminated food).

Glossary	Definition
Detergent	Material for removing dirt during cleaning. Detergent soap and soaps differ in their composition but have similar action. They do not destroy micro organisms (see disinfectant).
Dirt trap	Any area which is capable of trapping dirt. These can be voids between pieces of equipment, cracks/joints in surface finishes, long pipework runs. Dirt traps need to be eliminated or given special attention during cleaning.
Disinfectant	A chemical used to kill micro organisms and reduce levels of contamination on food equipment or in food premises. Disinfectants used must be suitable for use in food premises.
Disinfection	The reduction in levels of contamination on food equipment or in food premises by the use of a disinfectant.
Due diligence	The legal defence, available in Section 21 of The Food Safety Act 1990, that a person took all reasonable precautions and exercised all due diligence to avoid commission of the offence.
Electric fly killer	Equipment to control flies and other flying insects. Insects are attracted by UV lamps and destroyed on a high voltage grid.
Eutectic plates	Plates or packs designed to be cooled in a fridge or freezer and then used to help keep food cool when it is kept in insulated containers.
Fly screen	Fine mesh screen fitted to windows or other openings to stop the entry of flies and other insects.
Food	Includes drink, ice, chewing gum, ingredients used in the preparation of food and substances with no nutritional value, which are used for human consumption.
Food authority	The authority who is responsible for enforcing the Food Safety Laws. This is usually 'the Council'.
Food business	Has the meaning assigned to it in the Food Safety (General Food Hygiene) Regulations 1995. It means any undertaking, whether carried on for profit or not and whether public or private, carrying out any or all of the following operations, namely, preparation, processing, manufacturing, packaging, storing, transportation, distribution, handling or offering for sale or supply of food.
Food contact surface	Any surface which comes, or may come, into contact with food, either directly or in such close proximity that it could contaminate the food if dirty (includes work surfaces, containers and equipment).
Food handler	Any person involved in a food business who handles food in the course of their work, or as part of their duties to any extent, whether the food is open or pre-wrapped.
Food hazard	Anything that may affect food which will result in harm to someone eating the food.
Food pest	Animal life unwelcome in food premises. Especially insects, birds, rats, mice and other rodents capable of contaminating food directly or indirectly.
Food poisoning	Illness transmitted by contaminated food. Food is contaminated if there is something in it which should not be there. Symptoms commonly include diarrhoea and/or vomiting, but many other effects are possible.
Hazard analysis	The identification of hazards, the steps at which they could occur and the introduction of measures to control them.

Glossary	Definition
High risk foods	Foods on which bacteria can easily grow, and which may be eaten without further cooking. High risk foods are usually moist and high in protein. Ready to eat foods are high risk because if they are contaminated or allowed to deteriorate, there are no further preparation steps to control the hazard. Examples include cooked meat and poultry, pates, meat pies, cooked meat products including gravy and stock, milk, cream, artificial cream, custards and dairy produce, shellfish and other seafood (cooked or intended to be eaten raw),cooked rice and cooked eggs and products made with eggs (e.g. mayonnaise) but excluding pastry, bread and similar baked goods, prepared salads, fruit and vegetables, soft cheeses etc. Cook-chill dishes and cook-freeze dishes are regarded as 'high risk' even if they may be served hot.
Humidity	Warm, damp air.
Hygiene	Measures to ensure the safety and wholesomeness of food.
Impervious	Incapable of absorbing anything (i.e. waterproof).
Induction training	Training given to new employees. Includes information on how the employee is to carry out their work hygienically. May be adequate in the short term and may precede more formal training.
Injurious to health	Harmful physical or mental effect caused by the consumption of food. Includes the probable effect, the probable cumulative effect and any individual reaction to a food. The injury may be temporary or permanent.
Intervening ventilated space	An enclosed area separating toilet compartments and food rooms which is mechanically or naturally ventilated to the external air.
Low risk food	Foods on which bacteria cannot easily grow or multiply. Includes dried/pickled foods, food with high salt/sugar content (e.g. bacon), jam, chemically preserved food, ambient stable foods (e.g. bread, biscuits). Food is also 'low risk' if it is raw and still has to be cleaned or processed as subsequent processing (e.g. cooking) should make it safe. Low risk food may transfer contamination to ready to eat foods and should be kept apart.
Lux	A measure of light levels.
Market/Fair operator	Those responsible for the organisation and/or operation of markets and fairs.
Micro-organisms	Any small living organisms (e.g. bacteria, yeasts, moulds and viruses).
Monitoring	Regular checks, to ensure a system is working properly. The results of monitoring are usually recorded in writing.
Mould	A microscopic plant which grows in damp conditions and surface of food but actually penetrates the food.
Non-absorbent	Any material through which water cannot pass.
Non-toxic	A substance which is not poisonous and will not contaminate food.
Open food	Food which is not in a wrapper or container which excludes the risk of contamination from the environment.
Pathogen	A micro-organism which may cause illness.
Perishable	Foods which spoil quickly or may be contaminated with bacteria which, if allowed to will multiply and cause food spoilage and/or food poisoning.
Permanent stall	A stall whose structure is not dismantled and the entire stock is not removed from the stall at the end of a trading period.

Glossary	Definition
Piping hot	Thoroughly heated to at least 70°C.
Private water supply	Water from a private well or spring rather than from the public mains.
Potable water	Safe to drink and acceptable for use in food preparation (i.e. drinking water).
Proofing (against pests)	Proofing of the structure of premises, especially doors, windows and the entry point of services/pipes, to prevent the entry of pests.
Probe thermometer	Thermometer attached to a probe which can be inserted into food to measure its internal temperature. Can also be placed between food packages to get a better idea of the food temperature rather than relying on surface temperature.
Proprietor	The person who carries on the food business. This can be either a manager or owner depending on their level of involvement in the food business.
Protective clothing	Should be appropriate for the work being carried out and should completely cover ordinary clothing. Where the sleeves are short, only clean forearms must be visible.
Reasonably practicable	Involves setting up a system of control having regard to the nature of the risks involved and depends on all the circumstances of the business being carried on.
Recognised Industry Guide	A guide which has been recognised by the Government as one which is presumed to comply with the Food Safety (General Food Hygiene) Regulations 1995. Enforcement officers must give due consideration to a recognised industry guide when assessing compliance with the Regulations.
Regularly/periodically	Means 'as necessary' and should relate to the build up of dirt or the rate of deterioration/wear and how this affects food safety. (Frequency can be determined through hazard analysis).
Sanitiser	Same as disinfectant. Combined detergent/sanitisers can allow a one-stage cleaning and disinfecting process.
Shelf stable	Foods which do not normally suffer microbiological spoilage at room temperature.
Sneeze screen	Screen, usually glass or another transparent material, attached to display area/cabinet to protect against direct contamination by the public.
Sterilised	When food is heated to a high temperature for a long time killing all the bacteria and viruses. The food is sealed in airtight containers. Chemicals can be used instead of heat.
Stock rotation	The practice of making sure that older supplies of food are used before new stock.
Temporary stall	A stall whose structure and/or stock from the stall is removed at the end of the trading period.
Toxic/Toxin	Poisonous substances. May be contamination from external sources (e.g. chemical spillage) or produced by the growth of micro-organisms.
Use by date	Date mark required on microbiologically perishable pre-packed foods. It is an offence to sell food after the 'use by' date.

ASSOCIATION OF PRIVATE MARKET OPERATORS (APMO)
4 WORRY GOOSE LANE
WISTON
ROTHERHAM S60 4AD

TEL 01709 700 072

BRITISH PEST CONTROL ASSOCIATION (BPCA)
3 ST JAMES' COURT
FRIAR GATE
DERBY
DE1 1BT

TEL 01332 294 288

CHARTERED INSTITUTE OF ENVIRONMENTAL HEALTH (CIEH)
CHADWICK COURT
15 HATFIELDS
LONDON SE1 8DJ

TEL 0171 928 6006

DEPARTMENT OF HEALTH (DH)
GENERAL FOOD HYGIENE TEAM
SKIPTON HOUSE
80 LONDON ROAD
LONDON SE1 6LH

TEL 0171 972 5071

ICE CREAM ALLIANCE LTD
5 PELHAM COURT
PELHAM ROAD
NOTTINGHAM
NG5 1AP

TEL 0115 985 8505

INSTITUTE OF FOOD SCIENCE AND TECHNOLOGY (IFST)
5 CAMBRIDGE COURT
210 SHEPHERDS BUSH ROAD
LONDON W6 7NJ

TEL 0171 603 6316

INSTITUTE OF MARKET OFFICERS (IMO)
21 TARNSIDE ROAD
ORRELL
WIGAN WN5 8RN

TEL 01942 827 975

LOCAL AUTHORITIES CO-ORDINATING BODY ON FOOD AND TRADING STANDARDS (LACOTS)
PO BOX 6, 1A ROBERT STREET
CROYDON CR9 1LG

TEL 0181 688 1996

MOBILE AND OUTSIDE CATERERS ASSOCIATION (MOCA)
CENTRE COURT
1301 STRATFORD ROAD
HALL GREEN
BIRMINGHAM B28 9AP

TEL 0121 693 7000

NATIONAL ASSOCIATION OF BRITISH MARKET AUTHORITIES (NABMA)
41 ST. JAMES' ROAD
ORRELL
WIGAN WN5 8SS

TEL 01695 623 860

NATIONAL MARKET TRADERS' FEDERATION (NMTF)
HAMPTON HOUSE
HAWSHAW LANE
HOYLAND
BARNSLEY S74 0HA

TEL 01226 749 021

ROYAL ENVIRONMENTAL HEALTH INSTITUTE OF SCOTLAND (REHIS)
3 MANOR PLACE
EDINBURGH EH3 7DH

TEL 0131 225 6999

ROYAL INSTITUTE OF PUBLIC HEALTH AND HYGIENE (RIPHH)
28 PORTLAND PLACE
LONDON W1N 4DE

TEL 0171 580 2731

ROYAL SOCIETY OF HEALTH (RSH)
38A ST GEORGE'S DRIVE
LONDON SW1V 4BH

TEL 0171 630 0121

SHOWMEN'S GUILD OF GREAT BRITAIN
GUILD HOUSE
41 CLARENCE STREET
STAINES
MIDDLESEX TW18 4SY

TEL 01784 461 805/6

Contacts

SOCIETY OF FOOD HYGIENE TECHNOLOGY (SOFHT)
PO BOX 37
LYMINGTON
HANTS S041 9WL

TEL 01590 671 979

THE SCOTTISH OFFICE AGRICULTURE, ENVIRONMENT & FISHERIES DEPT.
PENTLAND HOUSE
47 ROBBS LOAN
EDINBURGH
EN14 1TW

TEL 0131 244 6187

TITLE	AVAILABLE FROM	PRICE
ASSURED SAFE CATERING (BOOKLET) ISBN: 0113216882	THE STATIONERY OFFICE (TSO) PUBLICATIONS TSO BOOKSHOPS	£8.50
ASSURED SAFE CATERING (LEAFLET)	DEPARTMENT OF HEALTH PO BOX 410 WETHERBY LS23 7LN TEL: 01937 840 250, FAX: 01937 845 381 OR LOCAL ENVIRONMENTAL HEALTH DEPARTMENT	FREE
EC COUNCIL DIRECTIVE ON THE HYGIENE OF FOODSTUFFS 93/43/EEC OFFICIAL JOURNAL OF THE EUROPEAN COMMUNITIES No 175/1, 19 JULY 1993	TSO PUBLICATIONS TSO BOOKSHOPS	£10.25
FOOD SAFETY ACT 1990	TSO PUBLICATIONS TSO BOOKSHOPS	£7.10
FOOD SAFETY (GENERAL FOOD HYGIENE) REGULATIONS 1995 SI No 1763 ISBN 0110532279	TSO PUBLICATIONS TSO BOOKSHOPS	£3.20
FOOD HYGIENE TRAINING: A GUIDE TO ITS RESPONSIBLE MANAGEMENT (IFST1992)	INSTITUTE OF FOOD SCIENCE AND TECHNOLOGY 5 CAMBRIDGE COURT 210 SHEPHERD'S BUSH ROAD LONDON W6 7NJ TEL: 0171 603 6316	£10.00 (half price to members)
FOOD HANDLERS: FITNESS TO WORK GUIDANCE FOR FOOD BUSINESSES, ENFORCEMENT OFFICERS AND HEALTH PROFESSIONALS (A4 BOOKLET)	DEPT OF HEALTH P.O. BOX 410 WETHERBY LS23 7LN FAX: 0990 210 266	£2.50
FOODHANDLERS: FITNESS TO WORK GUIDELINES FOR FOOD BUSINESS MANAGERS (A4 BOOKLET)	DEPT OF HEALTH P.O. BOX 410 WETHERBY LS23 7LN FAX: 0990 210 266 OR FROM LOCAL ENVIRONMENTAL HEALTH DEPARTMENT	FREE

TITLE	AVAILABLE FROM	PRICE
FOODHANDLERS: FITNESS TO WORK (LEAFLET)	AS ABOVE OR FROM LOCAL ENVIRONMENTAL HEALTH DEPT.	FREE
HYGIENE FOR MANAGEMENT (SEVENTH EDITION) RICHARD A SPRENGER HIGHFIELD PUBLICATIONS 1995 ISBN: 1871912601	TSO AND OTHER BOOKSHOPS	£22.05
INDUSTRY GUIDES: A TEMPLATE	DEPT OF HEALTH P.O. BOX 410 WETHERBY LS23 7LN FAX: 0990 210 266	FREE
THE FOOD SAFETY (TEMPERATURE CONTROL) REGULATIONS 1995 SI No: 2200 ISBN 0110533836	TSO PUBLICATIONS TSO BOOKSHOPS	£2.35
INDUSTRY GUIDE TO GOOD HYGIENE PRACTICE: CATERING GUIDE ISBN: 0 900 103 00 0	CHADWICK HOUSE GROUP LTD. CHADWICK COURT 15 HATFIELDS LONDON SE1 8DJ TEL: 0171 827 5882 FAX: 0171 827 9930	£3.60
MOBILE CATERING GETTING STARTED (BOOK)	MOBILE AND OUTSIDE CATERERS ASSOCIATION (MOCA) CENTRE COURT 1301 STRATFORD ROAD, HALL GREEN BIRMINGHAM B28 9AP TEL: 0121 693 7000	£3.75 (PACK ALSO AVAILABLE WITH ADDITIONAL ITEMS £11.75)
MOBILE AND OUTSIDE CATERERS ASSOCIATION CODE OF PRACTICE	MOCA AS ABOVE	£11.75
NATIONAL GUIDELINES FOR OUTDOOR CATERING	CHARTERED INSTITUTE OF ENVIRONMENTAL HEALTH CHADWICK COURT 15 HATFIELDS LONDON SE1 8DJ TEL: 0171 928 6006	£6.00 (including p&p)
GUIDANCE ON THE FOOD SAFETY (TEMPERATURE CONTROL) REGULATIONS 1995	DEPT OF HEALTH ROOM 501a SKIPTON HOUSE 80 LONDON ROAD LONDON SE1 6LH TEL: 0171 972 5080	FREE

TITLE	AVAILABLE FROM	PRICE
A GUIDE TO THE GENERAL FOOD HYGIENE REGULATIONS 1995	DEPT OF HEALTH P.O. BOX 410 WETHERBY LS23 7LN FAX: 0990 210 266 OR FROM LOCAL ENVIRONMENTAL HEALTH DEPARTMENT	FREE
A GUIDE TO THE GENERAL TEMPERATURE CONTROL REGULATIONS 1995	AS ABOVE	FREE
A GUIDE TO FOOD HAZARDS AND YOUR BUSINESS	AS ABOVE	FREE
GUIDE TO THE SAFE HANDLING AND SERVICE OF ICE CREAM	THE ICE CREAM ALLIANCE LTD 5 PELHAM COURT PELHAM ROAD NOTTINGHAM NG5 1AP	£1 (1st copy free to members)